T0272530

A LIGHT FOR THE NATIONS

SERIES EDITORS

Pablo T. Gadenz
Mount St. Mary's University and Seminary, Maryland

Gregory Y. Glazov
Immaculate Conception Seminary School of Theology
Seton Hall University

Jeffrey L. Morrow
Immaculate Conception Seminary School of Theology
Seton Hall University

EDITORIAL BOARD

English translation copyright © 2024
The Catholic University of America Press

Originally published as *Una luz para las naciones: La vocación universal del Evangelio*
© 2014 Ediciones Universidad San Dámaso, Madrid

ISBN: 978-0-8132-3855-5
Paperback ISBN: 978-0-8132-3840-1
eISBN: 978-0-8132-3841-8

The paper used in this publication meets the minimum requirements
of American National Standards for Information Science—
Permanence of Paper for Printed Library Materials, ANSI Z39.48-1984.

Nihil Obstat:
Reverend Avelino Gonzalez, STD
Censor Deputatus

Imprimatur:
Most Reverend Juan Esposito, JCD
Vicar General and Moderator of the Curia

The Roman Catholic Archdiocese of Washington
August 14, 2024

The *nihil obstat* and *imprimatur* are official declarations that a book or
pamphlet is free of doctrinal or moral error. There is no implication that those
who have granted the *nihil obstat* and the *imprimatur* agree with the content,
opinions or statements expressed therein.

Cataloging-in-Publication Data on File at the Library of Congress

The translation and edition of this work has been generously financed
by the San Dámaso Ecclesiastical University, Madrid-Spain
(UESD OIRI Prot. N°. 2020–21; 2ª/3/2 and 2021–22; 2ª/3/1.).

Printed in the United States.
Book design by Burt&Burt
Interior set with Minion Pro and Astoria

A Light for the Nations

THE SCRIPTURES ON THE UNIVERSAL MISSION OF ISRAEL AND THE CHURCH

LUIS SÁNCHEZ-NAVARRO

Translated by
KRISTIN TOWLE

Foreword by
FRANK J. MATERA

The Catholic University of America Press
Washington, D.C.

"To this day I have had the help
that comes from God,
and so I stand here testifying
both to small and great,
saying nothing but what the prophets
and Moses said would come to pass:
that the Christ must suffer,
and that, by being the first
to rise from the dead,
he would proclaim light both
to the people and to the Gentiles."

(Acts 26:22-23)

*In memory of Pope Benedict XVI,
indefatigable evangelist, with gratitude.*

Contents

Abbreviations

AB	The Anchor Bible
ABE	Asociación Bíblica Española. Institución San Jerónimo. Monografías
ABRL	The Anchor Bible Reference Library
AmUSt.TR	American University Studies. Series VII: Theology and Religion
AnBib	Analecta Biblica
BAC	Biblioteca de Autores Cristianos
BBC	Biblioteca bíblica Cristiandad
BEB	Biblioteca de estudios bíblicos
BECNT	Baker Exegetical Commentary on the New Testament
BHB	Biblioteca Hispana Biblica
BibDial	Bible in Dialogue
BibPr	Bibbia e preghiera
BNot	Buena Noticia
BTC	Biblioteca de Teología Comillas
CBJer	Comentarios a la Nueva Biblia de Jerusalén
CBQ	*Catholic Biblical Quarterly*
CBQMS	Catholic Biblical Quarterly Monograph Series
CCC	*Catechism of the Catholic Church*. 2nd ed. New York: Doubleday, 2003.
CCTC	Cambridge Classical Texts and Commentaries
CMat	Collectanea Matritensia
CNT	Commentaire du Nouveau Testament
CP	Comprender la Palabra

CRB	Cahiers de la Revue Biblique
CSB	Collana Studi Biblici
CurBR	*Currents in Biblical Research*
EDIS	Edition Israelogie
EDNT	*Exegetical Dictionary of the New Testament.* Edited by Horst Balz and Gerhard Schneider. 3 vols. Edinburgh: T&T Clark, 1990–93.
EHS.T	Europäische Hochschulschriften. Reihe XXIII – Theologie
EKKNT	Evangelisch-Katholischer Kommentar zum Neuen Testament
EncJud	*Encyclopedia Judaica.* Edited by Fred Skolnik and Michael Berenbaum. 2nd ed. 22 vols. Detroit: Macmillan Reference USA, 2007.
EstB	Estudios bíblicos
GNS	Good News Studies
HTCNT	Herder's Theological Commentary on the New Testament
IBS	*Irish Biblical Studies* (Belfast)
ICC	International Critical Commentary
IEB	Introducción al estudio de la Biblia
JBC XXI	*The Jerome Biblical Commentary for the Twenty-First Century.* Edited by John J. Collins, Gina Hens-Piazza, Barbara Reid, and Donald Senior. With a Foreword by Pope Francis. London: T&T Clark, 2022.
LB	Lire la Bible
NBE.C	Nueva Biblia Española – Comentarios
NDTB	*Nuevo diccionario de teología bíblica.* Edited by Pietro Rossano, Gianfranco Ravasi, and Antonio Girlanda. Madrid: Paulinas, 1990.
NIBCOT	New International Biblical Commentary on the Old Testament
NICOT	The New International Commentary on the Old Testament

NJBC	*The New Jerome Biblical Commentary.* Edited by Raymond Brown, Joseph A. Fitzmyer, and Roland E. Murphy. Upper Saddle River, NJ: Prentice Hall, 1990.
NRTh	*La nouvelle revue théologique* (Louvain)
NTSI	The New Testament and the Scriptures of Israel
OTL	The Old Testament Library
PD	Presencia y Diálogo
PFTNE.B	Publicaciones de la Facultad de Teología del Norte de España. Sede de Burgos
RevAg	*Revista agustiniana* (Madrid)
RivB	*Rivista biblica italiana* (Brescia)
SANT	Studien zum Alten und Neuen Testament
SBLRBS	Society of Biblical Literature. Resources for Biblical Study
ScrTh	*Scripta Theologica* (Pamplona)
SNTSMS	Society for New Testament Studies Monograph Series
SP	Sacra Pagina
SubBi	Subsidia Biblica
TGST	Tesi Gregoriana. Serie Teologia
TKNT	Theologischer Kommentar zum Neuen Testament
TRE	*Theologische Realenziklopädie* (Berlin)
USEK.T	Université Saint-Esprit de Kaslik (Liban). Faculté Pontifical de Théologie
WBC	Word Biblical Commentary
WUNT	Wissenschaftliche Untersuchungen zum Neuen Testament

Foreword

I t is an honor to introduce Luis Sánchez-Navarro, Professor of New Testament at San Dámaso University, Madrid, where, in addition to his teaching duties, he is the editor of *Estudios Bíblicos*, one of the premier biblical journals in Europe. A member of the Disciples of the Hearts of Jesus and Mary, Father Sánchez is the author of ten scholarly monographs, a collaborator in three more books, and the editor of ten other volumes as well as many scholarly articles. Throughout his long and distinguished career, he has dealt with questions that are at the heart of biblical theology, such as the meaning of Jesus' Sermon on the Mount, Jesus' preaching about the kingdom of God, questions of marriage in the New Testament, and the Church as the body of Christ. Most importantly, he has focused on the interpretation of the Word of God for the life of the Church, as the readers of this volume will soon discover.

In *A Light for the Nations: The Scriptures on the Universal Mission of Israel and the Church* (*Una luz para las naciones. La vocación universal del Evangelio*) Professor Sánchez deals with an issue of biblical theology—the universality of the gospel—that touches on two of the most sensitive questions of our day: the relationship between inclusivity and exclusivity in contemporary society, on the one hand; and the relationship between Israel and the Church, on the other. The thesis Professor Sánchez proposes is that the vocation of the Church to preach the gospel to all nations is deeply rooted in Israel's vocation as God's peculiar and chosen people. He argues that the Church's vocation cannot proceed apart from a profound recognition and appreciation of Israel's unique role in God's plan of salvation because the election of Israel was never intended to exclude gentiles from God's promise of salvation but to provide them with the way to salvation.

Professor Sánchez develops his thesis in a clearly written, well-organized volume that is a model of biblical theology. He demonstrates how Torah, the Prophets, and the Writings were open to a universal salvation that was meant to embrace gentiles as well as the people of Israel. Then, building on this survey of Israel's sacred writings, he discusses Jesus' message of the kingdom in the light of Old Testament promise to show how Jesus' ministry to Israel prepared for and resulted in the mission of the Church to the gentiles. Next, turning to the writings of the New Testament, Professor Sánchez investigates the Gospels of Mark and Matthew, the Gospel of Luke and the Acts of the Apostles, the Johannine Gospel, the Pauline Letters, Hebrews, and the Book of Revelation to show how the salvation Jesus brought to Israel resulted in the proclamation of the gospel to the gentiles.

In his presentation of the New Testament writings, Professor Sánchez consistently deals with the many texts that, on first reading, appear to argue against his thesis—for example, Jesus' exclusive mission during his ministry to the lost sheep of the house of Israel according to Matthew 10:5–6 and 15:24, the hostility between Jesus and "the Jews" that occurs throughout the Johannine Gospel, the contrast between doing the law and believing in the gospel that plays such a central role in the Pauline writings, and the apparent displacement of the old covenant by a new covenant in Hebrews 8:7–13. As he works through the material of the New Testament, Professor Sánchez unfailingly respects these and other tensions. In doing so, he shows us how these difficult texts contribute to his thesis when they are read in a wider canonical context.

All of this brings me to the importance of Professor Sánchez's work for contemporary Western culture, which greatly values inclusivity. Indeed, if there is one value that stands out more than any others these days, it is inclusivity: the desire to include everyone and do away with systems and groups that exclude others. Given the value that contemporary society attaches to inclusivity, it is not surprising that many find it difficult to understand and appreciate what the Bible means when it speaks of God's election of a particular people. How can we speak of God choosing Israel or the Church? When we speak of certain people or a certain individual as chosen or elected by

God, are we not excluding others? It is precisely this question that Professor Sánchez answers through his careful exegesis. Yes, it is true that God's plan of salvation is not limited in scope to just one people or one nation. Yes, it is true that the gospel is meant for all. However, if this plan of universal salvation is to attain its goal, it must begin, paradoxically, with a particular people whom God chooses from whom a particular human being, the Messiah, Jesus the Christ, arises. For it is through this people, Israel, and its Messiah, Jesus the Christ, that God opens the way to salvation for all. Thus, the universal scope of the gospel begins with a particular people, and a particular human being. The paradox can be stated in this way: without the election of a single people there is no salvation for all. Accordingly, while contemporary culture is correct in valuing inclusivity, inclusivity does not exclude the election or choice of a particular people who live in a way that distinguishes them from others. Indeed, while the Church is exclusive inasmuch as one must believe in Christ as the universal Savior of humankind, her exclusivity is the paradoxical way in which salvation comes to all the nations.

The tension between inclusivity and election brings us to the relationship of Israel and the Church, Judaism and Christianity. As Christians become more conscious of the sinful history of antisemitism that has marred their past, they become more aware of how such antisemitism mocks the central message of the New Testament that Professor Sánchez clarifies for us. For, if the faith of Israel is the fertile ground from which the gospel of Jesus, the Messiah, grew, and if the gospel of the crucified Christ has broken down the barrier between Jews and gentiles so that they might be one, what room is there for hatred toward the people from whom the Messiah came?

Throughout this work, Professor Sánchez rightly insists that the Church is *not* the "true Israel" that displaces or sets aside the "old Israel." Israel is and remains God's chosen people, and St. Paul assures us that in God's way and in God's time Israel will be saved (Rom 11:25–29). In the meantime, Israel remains God's people, playing a vital role, even now, in God's plan of salvation. As for the Church, she is the daughter of Israel, a community in whom the promises made to Israel (as she understands them in the light of the paschal mystery) have come to fruition in Christ.

The readers of this volume will find a model of biblical theology in this book that provides them with a way to understand the central message of the New Testament: the universal meaning and significance of the gospel for all nations. For, while Professor Sánchez does not deal with every aspect of New Testament theology, he does lead us through the New Testament by focusing on what is central and important. In doing so, he presents us with a theology of the New Testament that is deeply rooted in Israel's scriptures, thereby showing us how "the New Testament should be hidden in the Old and the Old should be manifest in the New" (*Dei Verbum*, paragraph 16).

I am delighted that CUA Press has published this volume and introduced its readers to one of the most significant voices of biblical scholarship in the Spanish-speaking world today. May the publication of this monograph lead to a wider readership of Professor Sánchez's work and a deeper understanding of the Church's vocation to preach the gospel to all nations.

Frank J. Matera
Professor Emeritus
The Catholic University of America

Introduction

"Catholicity" (i.e., universality) belongs to the essence of the Church. The command to preach the gospel universally has obvious consequences: both the theological teaching and the moral teaching to which this gospel testifies are directed to all people of all times. In the third millennium of Christianity, a time in which diversity is exalted, this claim can appear scandalous.

In the pages that follow, I intend to demonstrate how this claim is deeply rooted in the ministry of Jesus, witnessed in the canonical Gospels, and also attested by the rest of the New Testament writings; all of these books show the universal openness of salvation as the fulfillment of Israel's Scriptures. I also intend to demonstrate how this openness does not reduce Israel to irrelevance, as one could perhaps hastily conclude. I am conscious of the vastness of the theme, which would require many volumes for an exhaustive study; in my current investigation I will necessarily proceed with just a selection of biblical passages. In this way, I hope to show how the aforementioned claim corresponds to the will of our Lord Jesus, and simultaneously to emphasize how it is in tune with the main trajectories of the Old Testament.

* * * * *

In the middle of the first century of our era, a group of Jewish origin emerged in the Roman Empire's eastern region. It distinguished itself by its revolutionary integration of the gentiles into its very heart. In effect, the group did not demand that they obey the Torah, which was fundamentally symbolized by circumcision and by keeping the Sabbath; instead, it developed new rites of initiation that, while connected with the frequent practices of first-century Judaism (such as the baptisms of purification), had radically new purposes.

Nevertheless, in spite of this novelty, the sect of "Messianics" (this is what "Christians" means) affirmed that it had not broken away from the patrimony of the patriarchs, the Wisdom literature, and the Prophets. On the contrary, it presented itself as the definitive realization of the promises inscribed in the history of Israel and testified by the Scriptures—promises that, far from being limited to the people of the covenant, were directed to humanity in its entirety. But what should we make of this claim? Is it an abuse, or does it on the contrary represent a legitimate interpretation of Israel's Scriptures? First, I will attempt to respond to this question. Next, I will point out some features of Jesus' ministry that show his intention to bring to all human beings the salvation revealed to Israel. Afterwards I will go through the principal writings of the New Testament in order to discover how they witness to the divine project of universal salvation, mediated by the chosen people.

* * * * *

This investigation originated in the catechesis titled "Christ and the Church" that the then pope Benedict XVI imparted on March 15th, 2006; it was the beginning of his first great catechetical cycle. Eight years later, I dedicate the original Spanish edition of this work to that great pope. Only God knows the importance that Joseph Ratzinger, afterwards Benedict XVI, has had for my vocation to the service of Holy Scripture. May these humble pages serve as a testament to my gratitude, always insufficient.

Luis Sánchez-Navarro, DCJM
October 22, 2014
Feast of Saint John Paul II

Note on the
American Edition

In a time like the present, where various events (such as the COVID-19 global pandemic, or the war that is currently bringing Eastern Europe to its knees) both manifest and question the unity of the human race, the universal scope of the proclamation of the gospel appears even more urgent. It is therefore a great joy to present to the American reader this biblical monograph, in which I intend to show how the universal opening of the gospel of Jesus Christ corresponds to the deepest demands of Revelation, as witnessed by the books of the Old and New Testaments.[1] YHWH's choice of the Jewish People, far from enclosing it in particularism, opens it to universality as "light of the nations" (Isa 42:6), according to the promise of blessing made to Abraham (Gen 12:3); all of humanity is called to live from that beautiful and fruitful light. I hope to be able to show it in these pages.

Without the encouraging friendship of the Rev. Kevin Zilverberg, Associate Professor of Sacred Scripture at The Saint Paul Seminary School of Divinity (University of St. Thomas, St. Paul, MN), the English translation of this work would not have seen the light of day. To him I express my deep gratitude. Thanks are extended to Ms. Kristin Towle, for her competent and enthusiastic translation work, and to Mr. John Martino, from CUA Press, who has expressed his interest and support for this project from the very beginning. Finally, Prof. Frank J. Matera, who has honored me for years with

1 Cf. Juana L. Manzo, review of *Una luz para las naciones: La vocación universal del Evangelio*, by Luis Sánchez-Navarro, *CBQ* 80 (2018): 154–55.

his friendship, has offered me valuable observations that have allowed me to better outline the work; I sincerely thank him for his generous foreword.

In addition, my debt of gratitude to the late Pope Benedict XVI remains intact.

April 9, 2023
Easter Sunday

A LIGHT FOR THE NATIONS

CHAPTER ONE

Salvation for the Nations in the Old Testament: An Overview

Before considering the testimony of the New Testament, we shall turn our attention towards the Old Testament. Firstly, we aim to verify that this collection of writings (which the Jewish tradition knows as the *Tanak*)[1] is not a closed and self-sufficient reality, but rather a reality directed to the future; and secondly, that it already contains in itself a clearly universal vocation.

A. THE OPENNESS THAT IS CONSTITUTIVE OF THE HEBREW BIBLE

The Tanak is not exhausted in referring only to itself, but rather it is open to a fulfillment that transcends it; in this we see a sign that Israel, the chosen people, does not exist for itself alone, but rather it carries in its heart a seed of universal openness. We can demonstrate this truth by going over some fundamental aspects of the principal parts of the Old Testament; to do this, we will follow the order of the Hebrew Bible.[2]

1. The *Pentateuch* ends at the threshold of the promised land. Abraham had lived in it as a foreigner (Gen 23:4), and now Moses, after guiding

---

1 *Tanak* is an acronym composed of the first letters of the three great blocks of the Hebrew Bible: *Tôrâ* (the Law), *Nəbî'îm* (the Prophets), and *Kətûbîm* (the Writings).

2 For this part, cf. Ignacio Carbajosa, "El Antiguo Testamento, realidad abierta," in *Entrar en lo Antiguo: Acerca de la relación entre Antiguo y Nuevo Testamento*, ed. Ignacio Carbajosa and Luis Sánchez-Navarro, Presencia y Diálogo 16 (Madrid: Facultad de Teología San Dámaso, 2007), 21–50, esp. 28–38.

the people from Egypt to the land of Canaan, will not succeed in taking possession of it; in fact, he cannot even enter into it (Deut 32:49–52). The conquest and the possession of the land will be delayed until the history of Joshua and the judges (cf. Josh 1:2–6); therefore, the promise made to Abraham of giving the land to his descendants (Gen 12:7), a promise that is gradually realized, still awaits its definitive fulfillment. "Abraham and Moses are the two great figures of the Pentateuch, but, nevertheless, they do not get to possess the Land; the fulfillment [of taking the land] is reserved for later."[3] A passage from the beginning of Deuteronomy reveals what we could call the *structure of the fulfillment of the promises*: "[T]he LORD your God has multiplied you, and behold, you are this day as the stars of heaven for multitude. May the LORD, the God of your fathers, make you a thousand times as many as you are, and bless you, as he has promised you" (Deut 1:10–11).[4]

In the desert, just before entering into the promised land, Moses testifies to the fulfillment of the promise made to Abraham (Deut 1:10; Gen 15:5; 22:17) and renewed with Isaac (Gen 26:4) and Jacob (Gen 28:14), but immediately he prophesies an ultimate fulfillment of that very promise. The people have multiplied exponentially in Egypt (cf. Exod 1:6–7), but this is also a sign of the fruitfulness that God will give them in the future. Therefore, the fulfillment of the promise is not definitive. God's promises can never be given in a definitively closed way; they are structurally open.

Other promises exist within the Torah, and they point beyond it. Such promises include the announcement that a descendent of the woman will crush the serpent (Gen 3:15), or the promise that Abraham will become the mediator of divine benediction for "all the families of the earth" (Gen 12:3). For their part, the legal codes (the Decalogue and the Covenant Code in Exodus, the Holiness Code in Leviticus, and the Deuteronomic Code in Deuteronomy) testify to a process of adapting the legislation of Israel to the historical situation of the people, which leads to the legislation being successively reformulated.

---

3 Carbajosa, "El Antiguo Testamento, realidad abierta," 29. Translations of works from Spanish, excluding the Bible, are original unless stated otherwise.

4 Unless otherwise indicated, biblical quotations are from RSV 2nd Catholic edition.

All of these facts, therefore, prevent us from conceiving of the Pentateuch as complete in itself. These books "are thrown open to the future, towards fulfillment, and at the same time they are the result of this future."[5]

2. *Prophets.* The "Former Prophets" of the Jewish canon (the "Historical Books" in the Christian canon) close with the failure of the promise: the people of Israel are exiled from the promised land and held captive in Babylon, the temple is destroyed, and the monarchy is abolished (2 Kgs 25; 2 Chr 36). Even after the return from exile due to the Edict of Cyrus, Israel would not return to being an independent kingdom until the Maccabean period. The Hasmonean dynasty, however, was not Davidic, so it cannot be seen as the fulfillment of the prophecy made about the great king (2 Sam 7). Furthermore, despite the reconstruction of the temple, the return to the land after the exile did not imply the fulfillment of the great promises of interior purification contained in Jeremiah 31 and Ezekiel 36; the activity of the postexilic prophets, who denounce the infidelity of the people, demonstrates this.[6]

The writing prophets illuminate this history of Israel and testify to the growing obstinacy and rebelliousness of the chosen people, to the point that they need a "new beginning" that goes to their roots. "That is when the announcement of something new (*ḥădāšāh*: Isa 43:19) and absolutely gratuitous makes its way into the prophets (before, during, and after the exile). . . . The content of this new thing . . . is a 're-creation,' that is, a powerful gesture of YHWH that changes its [Israel's] nature."[7] Here we find the great "prophecies of a new thing": a new covenant (Jer 31:31–34), and a new heart and new spirit (Ezek 36:26). Isaiah speaks of an "eternal covenant" that God is going to establish with his people as the fulfillment of the promise made to David (Isa 55:3). "It is more than evident that all these oracles about the future have introduced into Israel an expectation, a dynamic of hope, of straining towards the future,

---

5 Carbajosa, "El Antiguo Testamento, realidad abierta," 30. In effect, the redaction of Deuteronomy—a book that shows significant similarities to the prophecy of Jeremiah—is closely related to the religious reform of Josiah.

6 Cf. Mal 1:6–2:16; 3:6–12; Joel 2:12–17.

7 Carbajosa, "El Antiguo Testamento, realidad abierta," 32.

towards a fulfillment, beyond this collection of books. And it is equally evident that the return from exile does not fulfill these expectations."[8] Other later prophetic texts witness to this straining towards the future; the conclusion of Malachi is very significant: even though it looks back by intimating the fulfillment of the law of Moses, still it closes with a look towards the future, announcing the return of the prophet Elijah, prior to the Day of the Lord (Mal 3:22–24).[9]

3. *Writings.* The sapiential literature testifies to the tension between the "traditional" wisdom (Proverbs, Sirach) and the criticism of it (Job, Qoheleth). The Hebrew canon does not manage to offer a synthesis, which the (deuterocanonical) book of Wisdom will indeed advance: the immortality of the soul. But the human body, which allows human beings to be in relationship with each other, remains excluded from that reality of immortality. So the fundamental question of the suffering of the righteous remains open: the resurrection of the body (to which 2 Maccabees 7 clearly witnesses) will need to be integrated. On the other hand, in the sapiential tradition, Wisdom appears mysteriously personified, a participant in divine qualities and a mediator between God and human beings (Prov 8; Sir 24; Wis 7–9); this represents yet another element of openness. The Psalms, finally, are constitutively open, since as prayers they constantly need to be brought into the present moment.

The Hebrew Bible, our Old Testament, thus shows us an essential openness that manifests at once the grandness of these writings, which testify to the history of salvation, and their limitation, since they point beyond themselves. It is necessary to keep in mind this condition of the books of the old covenant, because in this condition is rooted the central theme that concerns us: the universal dimension of the saving plan of God, a plan that has the people of Israel at its center, but whose final realization goes beyond this people.

8 Carbajosa, "El Antiguo Testamento, realidad abierta," 33.

9 Regarding the expectation of the future kingdom in the Qumran community, grounded in the eschatological scope of the promises of Scripture, see Carbajosa, "El Antiguo Testamento, realidad abierta," 39–47.

B. The Universal Scope of the Old Testament

An attentive reading of the Old Testament allows one to understand that these books transcend the people that is their bearer through history. This characteristic is not imposed on the books from outside; on the contrary, it belongs to their very heart.

The particular relationship of the "Law, Prophets, and Writings" with the people of Israel is an evident truth that thus offers a point of departure. Scripture belongs to Israel: the people that has received the revelation to which these pages testify, the people that has assumed Scripture as the norm for its life, the people that has written it down and conserved it by transmitting it. These books give testimony of the covenant established by God with Israel: a covenant that God promises to be eternally established (cf. 2 Sam 7:8–16; Ps 89:4–5). The opposition that Scripture places between Israel and the nations, before which the chosen people must maintain the integrity of its identity, appears as a sign of the Lord's predilection for his people (cf. 2 Sam 7:23). Occasionally, however, it can give the impression that God's salvation, to which the Scriptures of the old covenant testify, is exclusively for Israel.

But along with the particular reference to Israel (which is certainly predominant[10]), the Old Testament reveals a universal openness of the salvation that God offers to his people, and this is from the very beginning of the Tanak. These references are not presented as marginal but rather as constitutive and inescapable. Therefore, Israel's Scripture contains at its core a fruitful tension between particularism and universality, which is manifested many different times; later I will present some fundamental facts that show the openness but do not dispel the tension, since, as we shall see, they do not contradict the particular call of Israel. I will do this with the conciseness that our purpose requires, aware that development of the theme would be very broad. Let us note at the outset that in each one of the three great blocks of writings that form the Old Testament, there is a biblical book in which universal openness

---

10 Cf. Paul-Eugène Dion, *Universalismo religioso en Israel: Desde los orígenes a la crisis macabea*, BNot 3 (Estella, Spain: Verbo Divino, 1976), 17–21: "Preponderancia de la elección sobre el universalismo en el Antiguo Testamento." The title of the original French edition of this book is significant: *Dieu universel et peuple élu* (1975) [Universal God and Chosen People].

is essential to its substance: Ruth (historical books), Jonah (prophetic books), and Job (sapiential books).[11]

B.1. The Pentateuch and the Historical Books

The Torah opens with the stories of creation (Gen 1–3). God appears as the creator of "heaven and earth," a saying that expresses the totality by mentioning the two extremes. If God is the creator of everything, then it signifies that he is the one and only God; at the same time, the affirmation of monotheism implies his universal power. In particular, man is presented as the origin of all humanity (Eve means "mother of all the living": Gen 3:20). And the sin of our first parents has consequences for all their descendants, as the episode of Noah will demonstrate (Gen 6–9).

1. The *first story of creation* (Gen 1:1–2:4a) is particularly revealing about the salvation that God plans for *all* people. Various aspects stand out in these initial pages of the Bible:

    a. The aforesaid expression "heaven and earth" frames the story in terms of *inclusio* (1:1 and 2:4).

    b. The story insists on the goodness and beauty of creation: it affirms seven times that "God saw that it was *good*" (Hebrew: *ṭôb*).

    c. The first human beings (Hebrew: *ʾādām*, "man"; Greek: *anthrōpos*), created "male and female," are in their unity made "in the image and likeness of God" (1:27).[12] This condition therefore affects all humanity, which descends from Adam.

    d. God's blessing and his giving of the land for human beings to use and have dominion over (1:28–30) are directed to this *ʾādām*, which in the first created man shows the unity of all human beings descended from him.

---

11 Ruth, the great-grandmother of King David, is a Moabite, not a Jew. Jonah preaches conversion to Nineveh, and the great pagan city responds in an exemplary way. Job is a gentile (from "the land of Uz").

12 See in this regard Carlos Granados, *El camino del hombre por la mujer: El matrimonio en el Antiguo Testamento*, EstB 49 (Estella, Spain: Verbo Divino, 2014), 22–23.

2. The third chapter of Genesis presents us with the history of the *first sin*; its consequences are also universal since they affect all the children of the first human beings. This chapter concludes with the human beings being prohibited from accessing the tree of life (Gen 3:24), but it also contains the first announcement of salvation for humankind (3:15).

3. The *story of Noah* appears as a consequence of the universal diffusion of sin (Gen 6:5–8); it shows the characteristics of a "new creation," and contains the first covenant of God with all human beings, the descendants of Noah (Gen 9).

   God's command in Genesis 1:28 ("fill the earth"), renewed after the flood (Gen 9:1), shows the diversity of the nations and races as something willed by him: all of the earth becomes filled with the descendants of the sons of Noah (Shem, Ham, and Japheth: Gen 10). Later Deuteronomy will say that God distributed throughout all the earth the "sons of Adam, establishing the boundaries of the nations" (Deut 32:8).[13] The existence of "the nations" thus belongs to the divine plan.

   We see, however, that this divine plan has been altered by sin, which is at the origin of the confrontations between the peoples. Adam and Eve, as well as the inhabitants of Babel, wanted to become gods; the result is discord. In the future, the nations will be synonymous with idolatry, which separates them from God, and with pride, which makes them opposed to each other. The episode of the tower of Babel (Gen 11:1–8), which in certain aspects renews the original sin (Gen 3), is the clearest manifestation of this discord.[14] God, however, will respond to this situation by calling a man, the son of Terah, a descendant of Shem: Abraham.[15]

4. With the *history of Abram/Abraham*, the road towards particularism is begun; to him will be promised a singular blessing, in the form of a unique and abundant offspring: "And I will make of you a great nation, and I will bless you, and make your name great, so that you will be a

---

13 Cf. Joseph Pierron and Pierre Grelot, "Nations," in *Dictionary of Biblical Theology*, ed. Xavier Léon-Dufour, trans. P. Joseph Cahill S.J., revisions and new articles translated by E. M. Stewart, 2nd ed. (New York: Seabury, 1973), 380.

14 Cf. Pierron and Grelot, "Nations," 380.

15 Shem, Arpachshad, Shelah, Eber, Peleg, Reu, Serug, Nahor, Terah, and Abram, with his brothers Nahor and Haran (Gen 11:10–26).

blessing" (Gen 12:2). Many families already existed on the earth after the flood (cf. Gen 10–11); Abraham's family served other gods, just as the other "nations" did, but only to Abraham did YHWH reveal himself, leading him to an unknown land and giving him progeny (cf. Josh 24:2–3). From this moment on, the biblical history concentrates on the lineage of this man, with a perspective, therefore, that is increasingly particular.

At the same time, however, the blessing promised to Abram is marked by a perspective that greatly exceeds the limits of a single people: "by you all the families of the earth shall bless themselves" (Gen 12:3). When God later changes his name (from Abram to Abraham), he will explain this change by saying, "I have made you the father of a multitude of nations" (Gen 17:5). In Abraham, therefore, the particular call and promise are joined with a universal blessing.[16] The repetition of this promise in key moments of the patriarchal history (Gen 18:18; 22:18 [Abraham]; 26:4 [Isaac]; 28:14 [Jacob]) keeps alive this universal vocation of Abraham's family.

5. Let us note, finally, that the *history of Israel* presents the nations in a complex way. On the one hand, they are adversaries of God, both on the political level (in their opposition to Israel) and on the religious level (in their idolatry); the conquest of Canaan is characterized by a nationalism that is characteristically theological.[17] At the same time, however, in the Pentateuch and the historical books (the "former prophets" of the Hebrew Bible), we encounter the matrimonial unions of foreign women with such eminent figures as Joseph, Moses, David, and Solomon; moreover, in these same writings various people appear who are far from the offspring of Abraham and who can consider themselves to be "the first fruits of the nations." Notable among them are Melchizedek, the king of Salem (Gen 14:18–20); Jethro, the father-in-law of Moses (Exod 18:12);

---

16 "From the beginning, a reign universal in its scope is envisaged for the blessing given to Abraham. The salvation bestowed by God will spread to the ends of the earth." Pontifical Biblical Commission, *The Jewish People and their Sacred Scriptures in the Christian Bible* (2001), § 64. Translator's note: translations of magisterial documents are taken from www.vatican.va.

17 Dion, *Universalismo religioso en Israel*, 27.

Rahab, the prostitute of Jericho (Josh 6:25); Ruth, "the Moabite" (Ruth 1:4); and Naaman, "the Syrian" (2 Kgs 5:17).[18] Apart from that, after the conquest by the twelve tribes, some groups of Canaanites stayed and lived with the historical Israel.[19] Universality affects even the temple: the holiest place in Israel, and dwelling place of the glory of YHWH, will have to be open also to the uncircumcised. This idea is underscored in Solomon's lengthy consecration prayer, a passage in which he asks God to hear the prayer of the foreigner so that all the peoples may know his Name and fear him (1 Kgs 8:41–43).[20] This openness, in the time of Israel's greatest national splendor, shows the extent to which the fortune of all the nations belongs to the chosen people's consciousness of their mission. Deuteronomy, whose final drafting can be placed in the second half of the 6th century BC,[21] will testify in a similar vein to the universalist dimension of the Torah of Israel (Deut 4:6–8).[22] In this historical context, the prophetic preaching will make the divine plan of universal salvation increasingly explicit.

B.2. The Prophets of Israel

The mission of the prophets (*Nəbi'îm*) is explained by Israel's covenant with the Lord: the prophetic denunciation shows its exigencies; the divine promise expresses its ultimate end. The prophets have thus received a particular mission directed to the unfaithful people, who are invited to return to the covenant that is so frequently broken, and afterward to the people bereft in exile, to whom a horizon of hope is opened. But despite the clearly

---

18 Pierron and Grelot, "Nations," 381–82. Ezekiel mentions "Noah, Daniel, and Job" as the proverbial just ones among the gentiles (Ezek 14:14).

19 Dion, *Universalismo religioso en Israel*, 28–29.

20 Though perhaps with a dose of exaggeration, there is truth to the claim that these verses represent "the most marvelously universalistic passage in the OT." Simon J. DeVries, *1 Kings*, WBC 12 (Waco, TX: Word Books, 1985), 126.

21 Dominik Markl, "Introduction to the Pentateuch," *JBC XXI*, 191.

22 "The law of Israel is presented here as a universal wisdom, which is in contact with the governing Intelligence of the cosmos. The precepts given to Israel can therefore astonish all peoples, because they are the expression of a wisdom that is in contact with creation." Carlos Granados, *Deuteronomio*, CP 6 (Madrid: BAC, 2017), 51.

particular perspective, there is no shortage of glimmers of universal openness in these books (even in the first writing prophets); God not only equi-
tably judges all human beings according to certain rules of universal scope
(in which Israel enjoys no privileges over the nations in this sense),[23] but he
also has a plan for the totality of the nations.[24] Let us focus our attention on
two books: Amos and Isaiah.

1. Near its end, the book of Amos contains an interesting prophecy that
    is polemical towards Israel, which confidently boasts about its elec-
    tion: "'Are you not like the Ethiopians to me, O people of Israel?' says
    the LORD. 'Did I not bring up Israel from the land of Egypt, and the
    Philistines from Caphtor and the Syrians from Kir?'" (Amos 9:7). In
    a provocative way the prophet compares Israel to the Ethiopians, the
    Philistines, and the Arameans—this is a unique passage in Scripture.[25]
    To a people that uses its divine election to conclude that it will not suffer
    disgrace, Amos proclaims the universal lordship of YHWH. God directs
    not only the history of Israel, but also that of all peoples, so that he can
    hold them accountable; Israel, which knows YHWH, therefore has a
    greater responsibility.[26] Israel, however, is not the only people who has
    known the Lord's solicitude: the other nations also know it, though they
    are traditionally enemies of Israel.[27] The God of Israel is not only the God
    of Israel, but also of all the nations.[28]

2. The book of Isaiah is of special interest for our question. We will focus
    on some of its most representative prophecies:

---

23 Cf. Dion, *Universalismo religioso en Israel*, 55–64.

24 Cf. Isa 14: 24–27. "This is the first testimony of that universal solicitude which, beginning
with Deutero-Isaiah, will be translated into the calls to conversion from 'all the corners of the
earth.'" Dion, *Universalismo religioso en Israel*, 66.

25 "Amos 9:7 does not have any parallel in the whole Old Testament; it is unique to the book
of Amos. It constitutes the most explicit and radical revelation of the universality of God." José
Luis Barriocanal, *La relectura de la tradición del éxodo en el libro de Amós*, TGST 58 (Rome:
Editrice Pontificia Università Gregoriana, 2000), 251.

26 Barriocanal, *La relectura de la tradición*, 242.

27 Barriocanal, *La relectura de la tradición*, 251.

28 Regarding the tension between the particularity of YHWH-Israel and the universal
relationship of YHWH with the nations, see Barriocanal, *La relectura de la tradición*, 255:
"The singularity does not exclude the universality, but rather it makes it possible."

a. The book begins with a prophecy of universal salvation (Isa 2:2–5), in which certain important themes appear that will run throughout the book of Isaiah.[29] To the mountain of the house of the Lord, which will be shown to be superior to all the other mountains and hills (symbols of idolatry), "all the nations shall flow . . . and many nations shall come" (Isa 2:2–3), which will mark the beginning of a universal peace ("nation shall not lift up sword against nation": Isa 2:4).[30] The promise to Abraham to turn him into a universal mediator of blessing is now concentrated in Zion.[31] In this way the peoples will learn the Torah from the Lord: this "teaching," the "word of YHWH," is destined to "go out" from Zion (2:3), something that will be important for the New Testament.[32] Universal peace will be established by God insofar as he is the universal judge (2:4).[33] In this plan, the faithfulness of the "house of Jacob" has an important mission; with its walking "in the light of the LORD" (2:5) it will precede the "nations" (cf. 60:3). "Thanks to the testimony of a converted Israel, YHWH will reveal himself, at the end of history, as the God of all the peoples, so that the nations will come to Jerusalem in order to follow the ways of God."[34]

All of this will come to pass "at the end of days," and thus belongs to the eschatological hope of Israel. This expression, in effect, "does not specify whether the events it introduces will take weeks, years, or centuries to come. It shares in a pattern that appears throughout

---

29 Chapter 1 of Isaiah functions as the prologue to the book, and so Isaiah 2 represents the beginning. Francesc Ramis, *Isaías*, 2 vols., CBJer 19A–B (Bilbao: Desclée de Brouwer, 2006–8), 1:23. Cf. Isa 1:1 and 2:1. The prophecy of Isa 2:2–4 is also found in Mic 4:1–3. The themes are Zion and the temple as the center of the world; the confluence of the gentiles in Jerusalem; the Lord, light for the house of Jacob and for the whole world; and the eschatological peace. See Joseph Blenkinsopp, *Isaiah 1–39*, AB 19 (New York: Doubleday, 2000), 191.

30 Cf. Ramis, *Isaías*, 1:68.

31 Cf. John Goldingay, *Isaiah*, NIBCOT 13 (Peabody, MA: Hendrickson, 2001), 43.

32 Cf. Luke 24:47; John 4:22 (Ramis, *Isaías*, 1:69).

33 "The description of eschatological rule is not part of a human social program; indeed, the demonic threat of a return to war remains still virulent (Joel 4:9ff. = ET 3:9ff.). Rather, 'the holy city, New Jerusalem descends out of heaven from God as a bride adorned for her husband' (Rev 21:2)." Brevard S. Childs, *Isaiah*, OTL (Louisville, KY: John Knox, 2001), 31.

34 Ramis, *Isaías*, 1:68.

Scripture. Zion itself saw some fulfillment of this vision in OT times. It saw further fulfillment through the coming of Jesus and specifically through Pentecost. It still awaits complete fulfillment, as hinted by Romans 11:12."[35]

b. In chapter 19 of the book, we find a passage known as "the march of the pagans" (Isa 19:16–25).[36] After a threatening prophecy against Egypt (19:1–15) we see a radical change in perspective, since an amazing promise follows: "in that day" there will be in this land five cities that will judge according to the Lord (v. 18); there will be an altar of the Lord in the midst of Egypt (v. 19); "the LORD will make himself known to the Egyptians; and the Egyptians will know the LORD in that day" (v. 21). Furthermore, Egypt and Assyria, the secular enemies of Israel, will be united in the worship of YHWH (v. 23), to the point that "Israel will be the third with Egypt and Assyria, a blessing in the midst of the earth, whom the LORD of hosts has blessed, saying, 'Blessed be Egypt my people, and Assyria the work of my hands, and Israel my heritage'" (v. 25). "To call Egypt 'ammî (my people) is unheard of and promising."[37] The great prophet presents this encouraging future as the fulfillment of the universal mission of Israel: "When all of Israel has been converted to the Lord it will become the saving mediator of all humanity, and this is reflected in the symbolism of Egypt and Assyria, a metaphor for the pagan nations converted to the Lord."[38]

c. Later, in the middle of the "apocalypse of Isaiah" (Isa 24–27), we read a hopeful description of the salvation that will be accomplished on

35 Goldingay, *Isaiah*, 42.

36 Regarding this passage see Dion, *Universalismo religioso en Israel*, 157–63; Mario Cimosa, "Pueblo/Pueblos," *NDTB*, 1579–80.

37 Luis Alonso Schökel and Cecilia Carniti, *Salmos: Traducción, introducciones y comentario*, 2 vols., NBE.C (Madrid: Cristiandad, 1993), 2:1124.

38 Francesc Ramis, "El ocaso del mal: Is 19,16–25," in *Weodî ʿimmak: Aún me quedas tú: Homenaje a Vicente Collado Bertomeu*, ed. Juan Miguel Díaz Rodelas, Miguel Pérez Fernández, and Fernando Ramón Casas (Estella, Spain: Verbo Divino, 2009), 210.

Mount Zion (25:6–12).[39] The insistence on the totality of the peoples that are to benefit from salvation (vv. 6–7) compels one to count among them the traditional enemies of Israel as well, including Egypt (the original oppressor) and Assyria (a historical oppressor: see Isa 19, already discussed). The eschatological hostility against Moab (vv. 10–12) is explained by its symbolic character: it represents idolatry (cf. the lament over Moab in Isa 15–16), arrogance and pride, and, by extension, all wickedness.[40] In this way, the different scenarios presented by verses 6–9 and 10–12 are offered to Israel as well as to Moab and the rest of the peoples.[41] The ambivalent character of eschatological judgment (involving both salvation and condemnation) is in fact a recurring characteristic of the biblical message.[42]

Once these points are clarified, we can spell out the characteristics of salvation announced in the first part (vv. 6–8) of this important prophecy:[43]

i.   The eschatological banquet is characterized by superabundance: all the peoples come to the mountain of the temple to savor an extraordinary feast, in the context of a covenant. The description, in effect, evokes the meal that Moses, Aaron, Nadab, Abihu, and the seventy elders of Israel celebrated on Mount Sinai (Exod 24:11); and it also recalls the happiness that the Israelites experienced in offering worship in Jerusalem (cf. Deut 14:26).

ii. The "lifting of the veil" implies that all nations can come to know God.

iii. The annihilation of death, which is presented from the theological standpoint as a consequence of sin, is prophesied. This

---

39 In 24:23, Mount Zion is presented as the place from which "the Lord of the universe" will reign.

40 Ramis, *Isaías*, 1:229; cf. Childs, *Isaiah*, 185.

41 Cf. Goldingay, *Isaiah*, 144.

42 Cf. Isa 66:22–24 (conclusion of the book); Dan 12:1–2; Matt 25:31–46. They represent a problematic trait for the current culture: "In sum, the modern ideology of religious universalism, characterized by unlimited inclusivity, is far removed from the biblical proclamation of God's salvation." Childs, *Isaiah*, 186.

43 Cf. Ramis, *Isaías*, 1:228–29.

means, therefore, the definitive destruction of death and evil; the text subtly hints at the resurrection of the dead.

iv. Finally, the prophet announces universal consolation and the complete disappearance of all suffering: God "will wipe away tears from *all* faces" (25:8).

   All of these aspects will reach a new fullness in the New Testament revelation.[44] In a singular way, the description of the new Jerusalem in Revelation openly evokes the passage of Isaiah, in a universalist context of "the new creation" ("a new heaven and a new earth": Rev 21:1): "he will wipe away every tear from their eyes, and death shall be no more, neither shall there be mourning nor crying nor pain any more, for the former things have passed away" (Rev 21:4). The apocalypse of Isaiah is thus a prelude to the universal salvation—a salvation, let us note, that is intimately linked to Israel ("on this mountain": Isa 25:6).

d. Already in "Deutero-Isaiah" the figure of the Servant of the Lord appears: the one who is insistently alluded to as "a light to the nations" (42:6; 49:6). This mission is consistent with the universal call to conversion that we also read in this section of the book of Isaiah—an invitation that is based on the unicity of God[45]: "Turn to me and be saved, all the ends of the earth! For I am God, and there is no other" (45:22); this same prophecy declares the firm decision of YHWH, expressed in a judgment, to be recognized by all human beings (45:23).[46] Let us note, however, that if the songs of the Servant manifest with special emphasis the universal dimension of salvation ("a light to the nations"), they simultaneously present this salvation as being closely related to the covenant between Israel and YHWH:

---

44 "The Gospels evoke the feast in the parable of the nuptial banquet (Matt 22:2–10; cf. Luke 14:16–24) and in the Bread of Life discourse (John 6:51, 54); and they relate how all the peoples will arrive to sit down, at the end of time, at the table with Abraham, Isaac, and Jacob in the kingdom of heaven (Matt 8:11)." Ramis, *Isaías*, 1:229.

45 Cf. Deut 4:35, 39; 1 Kgs 8:60; Isa 45:5, 6, 14, 18, 21; 46:9; Joel 2:27.

46 Cf. Dion, *Universalismo religioso en Israel*, 108–10. "Deutero-Isaiah is the first biblical author that testifies to a religious universalism that asks for the conversion of all the peoples to the one God" (Dion, 122).

"I have given you as a covenant to the people" (42:6); "It is too light a thing that you should be my servant to raise up the tribes of Jacob and to restore the preserved of Israel" (Isa 49:6). By way of Israel's faithfulness to the covenant, all human beings are to be illuminated with the light of YHWH. Simeon, in proclaiming the infant Jesus as "a light for revelation to the Gentiles, and for glory to your people Israel" (Luke 2:32), recognizes him as the one who will bring to fulfillment this universal mission of the Servant.[47]

e. The universal horizon, finally, is clear in some prophecies of "third Isaiah." Already from the beginning he announces that the temple "will be called a house of prayer for all peoples" (56:7); this prophecy is rooted in the aforementioned visions (Isa 2; 25), which present Mount Zion as the pilgrimage destination for all humanity. Jesus cited these words of Isaiah in the cleansing of the temple (Mark 11:17 and parallel passages). "Jesus' action restores to the temple its identity as the House of Prayer and is thus a prelude to the establishment of the kingdom of God, because the conversion of the holy place into the House of Prayer is the culmination of the eschatological hope consisting in the reunion of Jews and gentiles in the temple announced by Isaiah's prophecy (2:2–4; 56:6–7)."[48] Furthermore, the people converted from paganism to the religion of Israel will be able to offer "holocausts and sacrifices" on the holy mountain (56:7); they will be able to participate fully in the temple worship.[49]

f. Later Isaiah announces the future splendor of Jerusalem, in which—again—the nations will participate (60:3–6).[50] The book closes with the same line: "I am coming to gather all nations and tongues; and they shall come and shall see my glory" (66:18); "And some of them

47 In Antioch of Pisidia, Paul will appeal to Isaiah 49:6 in order to justify the announcement of the gospel to the gentiles (Acts 13:46–47).

48 Ramis, *Isaías*, 2:253.

49 And not only through prayer, as the dedicatory prayer of Solomon foreshadowed (1 Kgs 8:41–43).

50 The theme of the nations that come to Jerusalem illuminated by the glory of YHWH underpins Isaiah 60, evoking the initial prophecy of the book (Isa 2:2–5). Childs, *Isaiah,* 496.

also I will take for priests and for Levites, says the LORD" (66:21);[51] "From new moon to new moon and from sabbath to sabbath, all flesh shall come to worship before me, says the LORD" (66:23). The conclusion of the book thus shows us a culmination of the universalist message of Isaiah and of the whole Old Testament, by contemplating preachers of the faith of Israel who even come out of paganism.[52] Let us note, though, that this universal horizon does not annul the function or the importance of Israel: "For as the new heavens and the new earth which I will make shall remain before me, says the LORD, so shall your descendants and your name remain" (66:22).

These passages selected from the book of Isaiah show us the salvation that God promises to his people as a benefit with universal consequences. Its influence on Judaism at the time of Jesus is immense, as the New Testament writings allow us to verify.

In conclusion, in the universal scope of the salvation that God has revealed to Israel, we recognize a fundamental element of the hope generated by prophetic preaching. "So, on the final day, a single people of God must be formed again which will recover once more the primitive universalism. Though the Law does give Israel an apparent exclusiveness, prophecy links back to the broad perspectives of the original mystery."[53]

B.3. The Wisdom Writings

Among the "Writings" (Kətûbîm) of the Hebrew Bible, the Wisdom literature stands out. Flourishing in the epoch of united Israel's splendor, during the reign of David and above all Solomon, who has become a figure of the wise in Israel, biblical wisdom shows us the fertile tension between universality and particularity;[54] to this I will dedicate the first part. The Psalms also belong to the "Writings" of the Tanak; because of the brevity that characterizes

---

51 Cf. Childs, Isaiah, 542.

52 Dion, Universalismo religioso en Israel, 131. "This is perhaps the closest anticipation of the Christian mission in the Old Testament."

53 Pierron and Grelot, "Nations," 382.

54 Dion, Universalismo religioso en Israel, 36.

our overview, and that makes just a selection of passages advisable, I will comment on two relevant psalms that exemplify biblical universality.

1.   In its very nature *the wisdom of Israel* shows a universal openness; the numerous points of contact with other traditional wisdom writings of the ancient East confirm this fact. Along these lines, it catches our attention that the protagonist of one of the most characteristically sapiential books, Job, is a non-Israelite (from the "land of Uz": Job 1:1).[55] Another book with a strong personality, Qoheleth, "the son of David, king in Jerusalem" (Eccl 1:1), reflects on the human person whose horizon goes beyond the chosen people, as can be concluded from the frequent expression "under the sun." And it is the case that every investigation of a sapiential type is in itself universal.[56]

In addition to this, there is another fundamental aspect: the wisdom of Israel is eminently anthropological.[57] Therefore, its scope transcends that of a particular people in order to treat of "man," with a perspective similar to the stories of creation.

> All the sapiential literature, by having man in himself as its unique center, offers a notable character of universality. Wisdom is for Israel a way of sharing with the other peoples what it has in common with them. "Wisdom" is the meeting place between Israel and the peoples, between philosophy and the history of salvation.[58]

But, once more, this does not contradict the genuinely Israelite character of this wisdom. The process is different: Israel discovers in

---

55 "This story serves to demonstrate the universal character of the biblical response to the problem raised by the suffering of the just." Maurice Gilbert, "Sabiduría," *NDTB*, 1716. "Job's experience is not specifically Israelite, but rather human and universal. The wisdom that is displayed and debated in the book is not the exclusive patrimony of one people, but rather wealth that is freely imported." Luis Alonso Schökel and José Luis Sicre Díaz, *Job: Comentario teológico y literario*, 2nd ed., NBE.C (Madrid: Cristiandad, 2002), 122. The location of this place is debated: is it in Edom? Syria? Arabia?

56 Maurice Gilbert, *La Sapienza del cielo: Proverbi, Giobbe, Qohèlet, Siracide, Sapienza* (Cinisello Balsamo: San Paolo, 2005), 241.

57 "The basic question for wisdom could be formulated in the following way: what is good for human beings? The human person constitutes the point of departure, the foundation, and the ultimate purpose of the efforts of wisdom." Víctor Morla Asensio, *Libros sapienciales y otros escritos*, IEB 5 (Estella, Spain: Verbo Divino, 1994), 82.

58 Cimosa, "Pueblo/Pueblos," 1580.

God's revelation a way of knowing that is valid for all human beings; in fact some Old Testament passages identify the Torah (which could be translated as "revelation") with wisdom.[59] Ultimately, only the openness to transcendence (where Wisdom dwells) confers wisdom and discernment on the human person; as the fundamental maxim reads, "the fear of the LORD is the beginning of wisdom."[60] The faith that receives revelation becomes capable of knowing human beings; biblical wisdom represents an authentic humanism.[61]

2.   The *Psalms* are in a way "a Bible within the Bible," for within them we find a recapitulation of the various ways of approaching the mystery of God and of Israel (historical, prophetic, sapiential), as well as the great themes of biblical revelation. They, therefore, also serve as a privileged testimony to the universal vocation of the chosen people. There could be many examples; we can focus on two, which are particularly important.

   a.   *Psalm 47 (LXX 46)*: from the beginning of this "liturgy of enthronement" of YHWH, all the peoples are invited to be united in the celebration: "Clap your hands, all peoples! Shout to God with loud songs of joy!" (v. 1). The perspective is very broad; "only Psalm 148 will exceed it, expanding the invitation to the whole cosmos, the heavens and the earth."[62] The universal dimension of the God of Israel is insisted upon: "the Most High" is "a great king over all the earth" (v. 3); "God reigns over the nations" (v. 8). In this context it becomes difficult to understand the historical, and strongly "national," motivation at first glance ("He subdued peoples under us . . . He chose our heritage for us": vv. 3–4); but "universal dominion is the horizon of election; only he who is the lord of all can prefer and elect one."[63]

---

59 Deut 4:5–6; Sir 24:23. "The *Tôrāh* revealed to mankind is also the organizing principle of the created universe. In observing that Law, believing Jews found therein their joy and their blessings, and participated in the universal creative wisdom of God. This wisdom revealed to the Jewish people is superior to the wisdom of the nations (Deut 4:6, 8), in particular to that of the Greeks (Bar 4:1–4)." Pontifical Biblical Commission, *The Jewish People*, § 43.

60 Morla Asensio, *Libros sapienciales*, 84. Prov 9:10; Ps 111:10. Cf. Prov 1:7; Sir 1:18, 27; 19:20; 21:11.

61 Gerhard von Rad, *Wisdom in Israel*, trans. James D. Martin (Norwich, UK: SCM Press, 1972), 307–19.

62 Alonso Schökel and Carniti, *Salmos*, 1:670. "Undoubtedly the invitation has a great deal of desire, plenty of hyperbole, and something utopian."

63 Alonso Schökel and Carniti, *Salmos*, 1:671.

The conclusion of the psalm evokes the universal vocation of Abraham; while Jacob (v. 4) refers to the chosen people, Abraham opens up to a universal horizon, capable of integrating "the princes of the peoples" (v. 9).[64]

b. *Psalm 87 (LXX 86)*: the universal perspective of this psalm evokes the same thing that is concluded from Isaiah 2:2–5, but it goes further. In Isaiah the peoples come to Zion from the outside, being foreigners, while in Psalm 87 "the Egyptians, Babylonians, Philistines, Tyrians, and Ethiopians are citizens with full rights,"[65] for they have been "born in it"—in the holy city (v. 4). This relates to the beginning of the psalm: given that God has founded Zion, the city of God (cf. Isa 14:32), it has a universal vocation.[66] God's promise to Abraham is concentrated in the holy city in a way: "I have made you the *father* of a multitude of nations" (Gen 17:5).[67] Now, the holy city is the *mother* of the nations.[68]

One's place of birth is not a secondary and contingent fact; it symbolizes one's true membership. We have a case that is contrary to this psalm in Ezekiel's accusation directed at Jerusalem: "Your origin and your birth are of the land of the Canaanites; your father was an Amorite, and your mother a Hittite" (Ezek 16:3). Unfaithful Israel is like a foreigner;[69] on the other hand, the vision of Psalm 87 represents the nations, eschatologically purified, as citizens of the covenant with full rights.

> They were born there and therefore they are citizens without distinction. They are not foreigners (*nkr*) or immigrants (*gr*) or inhabitants subjugated for work (2 Sam 8); they are simply citizens. Various texts speak of foreigners "incorporated" into the

---

64 Cf. Paul Beauchamp, *Hablar de Escrituras santas: Perfil del lector actual de la Biblia* (Barcelona: Herder, 1989), 124–25.

65 Alonso Schökel and Carniti, *Salmos*, 2:1123. Cf. also Isaiah 19:23 (on Egypt and Assyria).

66 "Since it is the city of the one true God, it will have a universal destiny." Alonso Schökel and Carniti, *Salmos*, 2:1127.

67 Alonso Schökel and Carniti, *Salmos*, 2:1125.

68 Cf. Gal 4:26.

69 A central theme of prophetic preaching is the circumcision of the heart: Deut 10:16; Jer 4:4. The true Israelite is not only marked by the covenant in flesh but also in heart (cf. Rom 2:29).

people of Israel (for example, Isa 14:1; 56:3, 6: later texts). Zechariah 2:11 is much closer: "And many nations shall join themselves to the LORD in that day, and shall be my people." Psalm 87 goes further.[70]

Later, in the New Testament context, we will have the opportunity to consider other psalms in which the universal call of the chosen people is reflected. Let us note again that this horizon does not erase the particular vocation of Israel, but on the contrary, this universality is built on the particular call.

B.4. Conclusion

All these considerations demonstrate the "universal call" of the salvation revealed to Israel and attested in the Tanak. Its strongly particular character (the Scriptures *of Israel*) contains a universal projection that is not ancillary, but essential. "Israelite universalism is that of a chosen people that is conscious of the universality of God."[71] Paul Beauchamp boldly states the following:

> There are therefore some reasons, based on the biblical language and beginning with the example of Solomon (who is at times good and at other times bad), to express things thus: Israel needs the nations as man needs woman . . . This means that Israel dies if it is only recognized in itself. Such is the law of the people of God. The life of that people that saw itself as favored with election will again end up in death if it does not also achieve the recognition of the universal, which does not depend on it. This recognition is what the Psalms call "the praise of the nations."[72]

Let us note, however, something that I have indicated in each part of this chapter: its openness to all the nations will not annul Israel or turn Israel into a useless reality. The people of Israel will not be a dead thing of glorious memory that has given way to a new subject of the covenant, but rather it will be called to be an active mediator of salvation.

---

70 Alonso Schökel and Carniti, *Salmos*, 2:1127.

71 Dion, *Universalismo religioso en Israel*, 13.

72 Beauchamp, *Hablar de Escrituras santas*, 124.

CHAPTER TWO

The Manifestation of Jesus

D uring the reign of Herod Antipas in Galilee, in a time of elevated messianic expectation in Israel,[1] a teacher characterized by a new way of preaching and acting will arise: Jesus of Nazareth. The novelty is such that, with great poetic force, the first evangelist presents him as a true "dawn"—as attested by Scripture—in "Galilee of the gentiles" (Matt 4:12–16); this prophetic reference, as we shall see, insinuates from the beginning of Jesus' public ministry the universality of his mission.

1. A singular prophetic figure, according to the unanimous testimony of the evangelists, precedes him: John, son of Zechariah, who will be called "the Baptist" because of the principal task he carries out; his evangelical presentation already transcends the limits of Israel.

2. Also the central motive of Jesus' preaching, the kingdom of God, suggests a very broad horizon.

3. Furthermore, among the actions of Jesus stands out an act with strongly symbolic content: the election of the Twelve.

4. Finally, the prophetic theme of the salvation of the gentiles is situated at the very heart of Jesus' preaching.

All these elements provide a prelude to the universal reach of the ministry of the rabbi from Nazareth.

---

1 The beginning of the Fourth Gospel, with the questions about John's identity, reflects this with particular intensity (John 1:19–24).

A. JOHN, THE PRECURSOR

The four evangelists open their narration of Jesus' public life with John the Baptist's ministry (cf. Acts 10:37); and all of them present it in relation to the initial prophecy of second Isaiah: "A voice cries: 'In the wilderness prepare the way of the LORD, make straight in the desert a highway for our God'" (Isa 40:3).[2] In this passage the prophet announces the imminent return from the exile in Babylon and describes it as a new exodus; it is therefore a *derash* (an interpretation that applies a passage to the present time) of the exodus event.[3] At the same time it is tinted with the universalism that fills this whole section of the book of Isaiah: "And the glory of the LORD shall be revealed [cf. Exod 24:16], and all flesh shall see it together, for the mouth of the LORD has spoken" (Isa 40:5). Redeemed Israel will reflect the glory of God before all the nations.[4]

This passage of Isaiah will be interpreted using a *derash*, even within the Old Testament, through Malachi's prophecy.[5] Here the one who prepares the way of the Lord (the same expression as in Isaiah 40:3) is an individual: "Behold, I send my messenger to prepare the way before me, and the Lord whom you seek will suddenly come to his temple" (Mal 3:1). The conclusion of Malachi's prophecy names this messenger that the Lord will send: "Behold, I will send you Elijah the prophet before the great and terrible day of the Lord comes" (Mal 4:5; cf. 2 Kgs 2:11).[6] This explains the expectation of the coming of Elijah at the time of Jesus, as the Gospels attest (John 1:21; Matt 17:10 // Mark 9:11).[7]

---

2 Matt 3:3; Mark 1:3; Luke 3:4; John 1:23.

3 "In Jerusalem, the disciples of Second Isaiah redacted the teacher's preaching and told of the return to Jerusalem by way of a second Exodus. Therefore, the content of 40:3–5 suggests the return of the deported by evoking the themes referring to the exit of the Israelites enslaved in Egypt." Ramis, *Isaías*, 2:49. Regarding the interpretive technique of *deraš*, see Domingo Muñoz León, *Derás: Los caminos y sentidos de la palabra divina en la Escritura. Parte I: Derás targúmico y Derás neotestamentario*, BHB 12 (Madrid: CSIC, 1987).

4 Ramis, *Isaías*, 2:51.

5 His prophetic activity occurred around the middle of the 5th century (circa 450 BC).

6 Andrew E. Hill, *Malachi*, AB 25D (New York: Doubleday 1998), 383.

7 Cf. also Matt 11:14; Matt 16:14 // Mark 8:28 // Luke 9:19; Matt 27:47, 49 // Mark 15:35–36; Mark 6:15 // Luke 9:8. Outside of the Gospels, Elijah appears only twice in the New Testament (Rom 11:2; Jas 5:17).

The Synoptic Gospels present the Baptist in the double light of Isaiah 40:3 and Malachi 3:1, and this explains why they speak of John as the "Elijah who was to come."[8] Particularly striking is the Gospel of Luke, which from its first page affirms that the son of Zechariah will go before the Lord "in the spirit and power of Elijah, to turn the hearts of the fathers to the children" (Luke 1:17; cf. Mal 4:6; Sir 48:10). Therefore, this presentation of John is related to the theme of our book, since in this Gospel, from the first preaching of Jesus, the figure of Elijah appears as a sign of the universality of God's salvation: Jesus will remind the inhabitants of Nazareth that the Tishbite prophet of Gilead was not sent to any widow in Israel but rather to the widow of Zarephath, "in the land of Sidon" (Luke 4:26; cf. 1 Kgs 17:9–10). We can thus glimpse the extent of the Baptist's mission, which is the prelude to the mission of him whose way the Baptist has come to prepare.[9]

B. The Gospel of the Kingdom

The beginnings of Jesus' preaching are characterized by the conjunction of two motifs: the *gospel* and the *kingdom of God*. Through their biblical undertones, both show a universal openness.

1. The first three Gospels designate the preaching and the very event of Jesus as *gospel* (good news). *Euangelion* (in Matt 4 times, Mark 8, Luke 0, John 0) is a term that is almost nonexistent in Old Testament Greek, where it appears only once (in a military context: 2 Sam 4:10). But the derivative verb, *euangelizomai* (in Matt 1 time, Mark 0, Luke 10, John 0) has undergone a specifically Jewish development: the Septuagint translators used it to translate the Hebrew *biśśēr*, "to announce good news."[10] The proclamation of Jesus will thus appear to his contemporaries as the definitive announcement from God, the Lord of history, according to the common usage of *euangelion* in Hellenism (news referring to the emperor), but its significance appears in all its profundity only through recourse to the Old Testament.

8 Matt 11:10; Mark 1:2; Luke 7:27.

9 In the Prologue of the Fourth Gospel, we are told that John's mission is "that all might believe through him" (John 1:7), so that from the beginning we recognize a universal reach.

10 The verb will appear more than forty times in the New Testament.

Some passages of Isaiah in which the verb is used are particularly notable: Isa 40:9; 52:7; 61:1. Given their importance for the Synoptic tradition, we will focus on the last two passages.

a.   The announcement in Isaiah 52:7 is uniquely important within the prophetic book, since it belongs to a prophecy (52:7–12) that in a certain way synthesizes the entire book.[11] In particular it interests us because it relates the "gospel" to the kingdom of God: it speaks two times of the mysterious messenger as an "evangelizer," and the content of that message is the kingdom of God. "How beautiful upon the mountains are the feet of him who brings good tidings, who announces [*euangelizomenos*: LXX] peace, who brings good tidings of good, who announces [*euangelizomenos*: LXX] salvation, who says to Zion, 'Your God reigns!'" (Isa 52:7)[12]

In this passage we find the undercurrent that illuminates Jesus' first announcement of the "gospel of the Kingdom" (Matt 4:17, 23; cf. Mark 1:14–15). The connection with Jesus' ministry is found to be even deeper if—as Francesc Ramis suggests—we relate the work of this anonymous messenger with the mission of the Servant of YHWH.[13]

b.   The prophet who later is presented as anointed by the Spirit and as an "evangelizer" (Isa 61:1) appears in continuity with the "messenger" of Isaiah 52:7; like him, the prophet evokes the figure of the Servant, but also that of the Messiah born from the stump of Jesse (Isa 11:2).[14] This prophecy is thus in continuity with the hope of salvation that runs through the entire book.[15]

---

11 "It is situated, practically speaking, in the middle of chapters 40–66; and, in this sense, it emphasizes the theological objective of Second and Third Isaiah and, by analogy, of the whole book of Isaiah." Ramis, *Isaías*, 2:210.

12 The NAB uses "announces," which appears twice (the RSV uses "publishes"). The Greek word *euangelizomai* means "to announce good [news]."

13 Ramis, *Isaías*, 2:212. According to his interpretation, this figure is a metaphor for the Remnant of Israel (Ramis, 88–89).

14 John N. Oswalt, *The Book of Isaiah: Chapters 40–66*, NICOT (Grand Rapids, MI: Eerdmans, 1998), 562–63; Ramis, *Isaías*, 2:304.

15 "Third Isaiah makes the theme of First and Second Isaiah concrete and deepens it." Ramis, *Isaías*, 2:247.

In Jesus' initial preaching, the prophecy of Isaiah 61 plays an important role: it is at the foundation of the Beatitudes;[16] Jesus alludes to it in Matt 11:5 // Luke 7:22; and, according to Luke, it is cited extensively in his inaugural preaching (Isa 61:1–2a; Luke 4:18–21). The "gospel" is therefore intimately connected to the kingdom of God; let us briefly examine this concept.

2. The Synoptic Gospels present in a concordant way the *kingdom of God* as the principal component of Jesus' message.[17] His public ministry is inaugurated with a proclamation that this kingdom is definitively at hand; Matthew speaks three times about the "good news of the kingdom," uniting both concepts and thus synthesizing the *kerygma* of Jesus (Matt 4:23; 9:35; 24:14). We are therefore looking at a theme that forms the backbone of the Gospels.

The Gospels, however, never define the kingdom of God: they expect that the reader will understand what is expressed by it. To this end it makes use of a double key. On the one hand, the expression draws all of its depth from the light of the Old Testament (diachrony), which presents God as the king and shepherd who governs Israel's existence and who promises to reunite the people in the future.[18] The announcement of the kingdom thus definitively fulfills God's promises. On the other hand, the kingdom receives its meaning from the broad context of each Gospel (synchrony). The mystery of Jesus, as manifested in his words and in his actions, reveals the scope and content of this kingdom. Ultimately it is concentrated in his person: he is, as Origen said, its personification (*autobasileia*).[19] The reading of the Gospels therefore reveals the nature of the kingdom of God, definitively mediated by the Son.[20]

---

16 This is particularly true of the first three beatitudes. Cf. Luis Sánchez-Navarro, *La Enseñanza de la Montaña: Comentario contextual a Mateo 5–7*, EstB 27 (Estella, Spain: Verbo Divino, 2005), 51.

17 Cf. John P. Meier, *Mentor, Message, and Miracles*, vol. 2 of *A Marginal Jew: Rethinking the Historical Jesus* (New York: Doubleday, 1991), 237–39.

18 Ps 45:7; 46:7–9; 68:25; 73:12; 95:3; 145:1, 10; Isa 41:21; 43:15; 44:6; 52:7; Ezek 34:11–31. One can understand the whole history of salvation attested by Scripture, beginning with creation, as a narration of the royal dominion of God. Meier, *Mentor, Message, and Miracles*, 2:241.

19 Origen, *In Matthaeum*, 14.7.

20 Matthew 13:41 and 16:28 speak of the "kingdom" of the "Son of Man."

3. Returning to Isaiah 52:7, let us note that the theme of the kingdom of
    God appears, already in the Old Testament, to be linked to *universalism*;
    Psalm 96 thus presents numerous points of contact with Isaiah 40–55:[21]
    "Say among the nations: 'The LORD reigns!' Yes, the world is established,
    it shall never be moved; he will equitably judge the peoples" (Ps 96:10).

The universal reign of YHWH is the great message that must be com-
municated to the nations; this reign implies stability and peace for the whole
world. The universal reach of the salvation celebrated by the psalm is in itself
related to the "good news": *"Proclaim the good news* [LXX: *euangelizomai*]
of his salvation from day to day" (Ps 96:2b).[22] This eschatological revelation
of YHWH as the universal king contains a radical novelty (cf. v. 1) that all of
creation must celebrate with boundless joy (vv. 11–12).[23]

> The term is especially significant in Isa. 40ff., where the messenger comes
> to Zion to proclaim the worldwide victory of God which initiates the age
> of salvation (52:7). This declaration is not just human word and breath, for
> God himself speaks through it, bringing to pass what is said by his own
> creative word. Ps. 96:2ff. is to the same effect. The great eschatological hour
> has come, and the message of God's acts of power goes out to the nations.
> Indeed the gentiles themselves will proclaim it (Isa. 60:6).[24]

It is not strange, in light of all this, that the first Christians would see
the psalm as a prefiguration of the work accomplished by Jesus Christ. This
Christian reading has been consequential for the transmission of the text:
some Christian manuscripts and ancient Patristic witnesses testify to an

---

21 Cf. Hans-Joachim Kraus, *Psalms 60–150* (Minneapolis: Fortress, 1993), 255; Alonso Schökel
and Carniti, *Salmos*, 2:1233.

22 Isaiah 52:7 illustrates these words: Alonso Schökel and Carniti, *Salmos*, 2:1233.

23 "This *cosmic praise* . . . is described by the poet by using almost the whole lexicon for 'joy'
. . . A pure and total joy in the style of the *Canticle of the creatures*, a hymn of jubilation that
emerges from the whole being to God the Creator, King, and Judge." Gianfranco Ravasi,
Salmi 51–100, vol. 2 of *Il Libro del Salmi. Commento e attualizzazione* (Bologna: Dehoniane,
1985), 1007.

24 Gerhard Friedrich, *"euangelizomai,"* in *Theological Dictionary of the New Testament*,
abridged in one volume by Geoffrey W. Bromiley (Grand Rapids: Eerdmans, 1985), 234.

addition, "from the wood," which shows the Christological reading of the psalm.[25]

Israel's mission in this universal proclamation is worth noting. "The worship of Israel is governed by the signature of an eschatological, end-time enthronement of Yahweh; his 'sacral' limits have been extended into universality . . . From the particularity of the elect Israel, Yahweh emerges in universal revelation."[26] Again, the universalism of salvation is linked to the mission of the chosen people.

We can thus demonstrate how both themes (the good news and the kingdom) share the characteristic of universality. Israel's openness to the nations acts as a prelude to the *good news* of the *kingdom*, which opens the New Testament.

C. THE GROUP OF THE TWELVE

A detail from Jesus' ministry, attested by both the Gospels and Paul's letters, is the choice of the group of the Twelve.[27] It is an act that the Gospels themselves do not explain, but whose meaning becomes evident in a saying of Jesus preserved by Matthew and Luke, in diverse contexts. Matt 19:28 says the following: "Truly I say to you, in the new world, when the Son of man shall sit on his glorious throne, you who have followed me will also sit on twelve thrones, judging the twelve tribes of Israel" (cf. Luke 22:30).

The explicit relationship of the Twelve to the tribes of Israel is limited, within the synoptic tradition, to these passages.[28] They are, however, sufficient to confirm what could already be intuited in light of Scripture. The

---

25 "Say among the nations: The Lord reigns *from the wood* (*apo tou xylou*)" (Ps 95:10 LXX). Cf. Alfred Rahlfs, *Psalmi cum Odis*, 2nd ed. Septuaginta X (Göttingen: Vandenhoeck & Ruprecht, 1967), 31.

26 Kraus, *Psalms 60–150*, 255.

27 The Gospel of John only mentions them in John 6:67, 70, 71; 20:24; and the only mention in Paul is 1 Cor 15:5. Current research does not doubt the historicity of this symbolic action of Jesus. Jacques Schlosser, *Le groupe des Douze: Les lueurs de l'histoire*, LB 184 (Paris: Cerf, 2014), 69–70.

28 See also Rev 21:12–14 (the twelve tribes of the sons of Israel and the twelve apostles of the Lamb). In various Old Testament passages, one finds (with small variations) the expression "twelve according to the number of the tribes of Israel" (Josh 4:5; 1 Kgs 18:31; Ezra 6:17; Sir 45:11).

constitution of the group of the Twelve expresses the roots of the Church in the Old Testament and at the same time confirms the trustworthiness of the promise.[29]

The twelve tribes form the fundamental structure of Israel; this reality runs through the whole Old Testament.[30] But the unity of the people loved by God was truncated, after Solomon's death, by the division into two kingdoms (1 Kgs 12). Moreover, a pivotal historical moment would arrive: the Babylonian Exile (6th c. BC), in which the chosen people were dismantled and dispersed. Then the prophets announce the restoration of Israel in the integrity of its twelve tribes in the future; see especially Ezek 47:13–48:29. The return from exile, however, would not see the fulfillment of this prophecy, for Israel's fragmentation persisted. Nevertheless, far from diminishing hope, this fact projects it into the future. In Sirach (2nd c. BC) we read this supplication directed towards God: "Gather all the tribes of Jacob, and give them their inheritance, as at the beginning" (Sir 36:11); the same Ben Sira affirms in another passage that Elijah was designated "to turn the heart of the father to the son [cf. Mal 4:6 RSV; Luke 1:17] and to restore the tribes of Israel" (Sir 48:10). The *Testament of Benjamin* also testifies to this conviction, near the time of the New Testament: "But in your allotted place will be the temple of God, and the latter temple will exceed the former in glory. The twelve tribes shall be gathered there *and all the nations*, until such time as the Most High shall send forth his salvation through the ministration of the unique prophet."[31] The extrabiblical literature thus shows the validity and the development of this concept among the Jewish People; in particular, the very name of the *Testament of the Twelve Patriarchs* testifies to how the consciousness of Israel's original constitution was kept alive.

Therefore, the institution of the Twelve, with its numerical reference to the twelve tribes and thus to the fundamental structure of the chosen people,

---

29 Schlosser, *Le groupe des Douze*, 84.

30 Cf. Schlosser, *Le groupe des Douze*, 84–92: "Jésus, les Douze et l'espérance d'Israël." Some notable passages are Gen 49:28; Exod 1:2–4; 24:4; 28:31; Num 1:44; 7:12–83; Josh 3:12; 24:1; 1 Kgs 18:31; 1 Chr 2:1.

31 *Testament of Benjamin* 9.2, in *Apocalyptic Literature and Testaments*, vol. 1 of *The Old Testament Pseudepigrapha*, ed. James H. Charlesworth, ABRL (New York: Doubleday 1983), 827 (emphasis added).

reveals to us Jesus' will to reunite Israel. It is not a distinct or *new* Israel, but rather Israel definitively restored. The people that was divided because of Solomon's sin (1 Kgs 11:9–13) and obliterated by Assyria (the Northern Kingdom: 2 Kgs 17:5–18) and by Babylon (Judah: 2 Chr 36:14–21) because of its infidelity to the covenant, will be restored in its integrity by the "righteousness" of Jesus (cf. Matt 3:15). A "logic of substitution" does not exist.[32]

> It is frequently stated that Jesus established the Twelve as the representatives of the new Israel, founding the new people of God with them. The expression "new people of God" is unfortunate; it does not appear in Sacred Scripture, which only speaks of "the new covenant." The constitution of the Twelve is therefore not directed to a new Israel, but to the new covenant with Israel. In some way we might understand this constitution in the sense that Jesus founds a new Israel because of the rejection experienced in Israel. Jesus' action is totally positive . . . With it he affirms that he is commencing the restoration of Israel.[33]

Therefore, the eschatological reconstitution of Israel in its twelve tribes is in unity with its universal openness, as notable prophetic passages allow us to glimpse. Ezekiel 39:26–28 presents an example:

> They shall forget their shame, and all the treachery they have practiced against me, when they dwell securely in their land with none to make them afraid, when I have brought them back from the peoples and gathered them from their enemies' lands, and through them have vindicated my holiness in the sight of many nations. Then they shall know that I am the Lord their God because I sent them into exile among the nations, and then gathered them into their own land. I will leave none of them remaining among the nations anymore.

Hence, we no longer have to understand the people of Israel as the exclusive recipient of God's salvation: now this people is eschatologically renewed, which allows all of humanity to access the salvation offered by the God of Israel. As Pope Benedict XVI teaches,

---

32 In relation to Jesus' affirmation in Matthew 21:43 ("Therefore I tell you, the kingdom of God will be taken away from you and given to a nation producing the fruits of it"), see below.

33 Klemens Stock, *Boten aus dem Mit-Ihm-Sein: Das Verhältnis zwischen Jesus und den Zwölf nach Markus*, AnBib 70 (Rome: Biblical Institute Press, 1975), 36.

As the system of the 12 tribes had long since faded out, the hope of Israel awaited their restoration as a sign of the eschatological time (as referred to at the end of the Book of Ezekiel: 37:15–19; 39:23–29; 40–48). In choosing the Twelve, introducing them into a communion of life with himself and involving them in his mission of proclaiming the kingdom in words and works (cf. Mark 6:7–13; Matt 10:5–8; Luke 9:1–6; 6:13), Jesus wants to say that the end times have dawned, in which the People of God will be established anew, the people of the 12 tribes, which now becomes a universal people, his Church.[34]

According to the prophetic Scriptures, the messianic era will mark the beginning of the salvation of the nations: "At that time Jerusalem shall be called the throne of the LORD, and all nations shall gather to it, to the presence of the LORD in Jerusalem, and they shall no more stubbornly follow their own evil heart" (Jer 3:17); this time will be marked by the reunification of Israel: "I will take you, one from a city and two from a family, and I will bring you to Zion" (Jer 3:14b). In the first chapter we were already able to perceive the universal openness of Israel's Scriptures. Now we see that the universal mission is in unity with the eschatological reconstitution of Israel; it is therefore the sign that this renewal has reached its fulfillment.

The numeral twelve has to do with Israel, the people of God. The nation is composed of twelve tribes. In any case, Israel's existence as a nation of twelve tribes was perceived as the ideal state of affairs. This was true even of the time of Jesus, though most of these tribes no longer were in existence. There are numerous attestations of this awareness ... [These testimonies] also express the hope that, in the messianic time of the end, the people as a whole will be restored. The ministry of Jesus is likely to be categorized as belonging to this context of expectation. Jesus' circle of the Twelve symbolizes the turning to the nation of Israel as a whole, the promise of its reconstruction, its destiny for the salvation of the coming reign of God.[35]

---

34 Benedict XVI, "Christ and the Church," General Audience (March 15, 2006). The last sentence of the translation, erroneous in the official English version, corresponds to the German original: "… daß die Endzeit angebrochen ist, in der das Volk Gottes neu gegründet wird, das Volk der zwölf Stämme, das jetzt ein weltumfassendes Volk wird, seine Kirche."

35 Joachim Gnilka, *Jesus of Nazareth: Message and History* (Peabody, MA: Hendrickson, 1997), 183.

Upon choosing twelve men from his disciples to form a singular group with a specific formation and mission (Mark 3:14), Jesus gave an unmistakable sign that the end times were upon the chosen people, who had been humiliated but hopeful for so many centuries. The election of the Twelve thus illustrates the content of his initial proclamation: "the kingdom of God is at hand" (Mark 1:15).[36]

D. THE "PILGRIMAGE OF THE GENTILES"

A saying of Jesus, preserved by Matthew and Luke, has come to be called "the pilgrimage of the Gentiles." In Matthew it appears at the conclusion of Jesus' curing the Roman centurion's servant in Capernaum (Matt 8:5–13), and the context suggests the theme of the gentiles. In Luke it appears in connection with Jesus' response, en route to Jerusalem, to the question, "Lord, will those who are saved be few?" (Luke 13:23–30); in this version, the plural *you* referring to the Jewish interlocutors is compared to the *they* that designates the gentiles, the eschatological dinner guests. The *logion* reads as follows:

I tell you, many will come from east and west and sit at the table with Abraham, Isaac, and Jacob in the kingdom of heaven, while the sons of the kingdom will be thrown into the outer darkness; there men will weep and gnash their teeth. (Matt 8:11–12)	There you will weep and gnash your teeth, when you see Abraham and Isaac and Jacob and all the prophets in the kingdom of God and you yourselves thrust out. And men will come from east and west, and from north and south, and sit at table in the kingdom of God. (Luke 13:28–29)

Joachim Jeremias argued, in a brief but prominent 1956 essay, that these words of Jesus are rooted in a prophetic theme that we already know: the eschatological pilgrimage of the peoples to the mountain of God, whose principal expression is Isaiah 2:2–5.[37] Jesus' *logion* especially evokes a prophecy of Isaiah: "Behold, these shall come from afar, and behold, these from

---

36 Cf. Matt 3:2; 4:17; 10:7; Luke 10:9, 11.

37 Joachim Jeremias, *Jesu Verheissung für die Völker*. Franz Delitszch-Vorlesungen 1953 (Stuttgart: Kohlhammer, 1956). The English version is *Jesus' Promise to the Nations*, trans. S. H. Hooke (Naperville, IL: Allenson, 1958). Jeremias, *Jesus' Promise*, 55–73.

the north and from the west, and these from the land of Syene" (Isa 49:12).[38] All of these gentiles will participate in the eschatological feast of the people of God, represented by the three patriarchs; they will then be definitively incorporated into this people.[39]

So, Jesus' ministry entirely points to this event. As Jeremias shows with profuse biblical references, this event synthesizes all the expectations of universal salvation in Israel's Scriptures; it culminates in the feast of salvation on the universal mountain (Isa 25:6–8). In the first place, we see the teachings referring to the eschatological feast, but we also find his instruction regarding the convergence of all people on Mount Zion, the eschatological gathering of God's flock, and the influx of people into the new temple.[40] The great German exegete offers the following summary:

> Thus we see that the incorporation of the Gentiles in the kingdom of God promised by the prophets, was expected and announced by Jesus as God's *eschatological act of power, as the great final manifestation of God's free grace.* For the last time God brings life out of death, creates children to Abraham out of stones, when in the hour of final revelation he summons the nations to Zion, and by constituting the universal people of God from Jews and Gentiles abolishes all earthly distinctions.[41]

Since Jeremias published his essay, the reactions have been numerous and diverse.[42] Let us limit ourselves to observing that, although a consensus has not yet been reached, "an emerging view is that the salvation of the gentiles was intimately bound up with the restoration of Israel."[43] Although the eschatological future of the other nations was a matter of speculation

---

38 Jeremias, *Jesus' Promise*, 62. Cf. Ps 98:3: "All the ends of the earth have seen the victory of our God."

39 "Earthly distinctions have disappeared. They drink of the water of life, and their hunger is appeased by the vision of the Shechinah." Jeremias, *Jesus' Promise*, 63.

40 Jeremias, *Jesus' Promise*, 64–68.

41 Jeremias, *Jesus' Promise*, 70–71.

42 Michael F. Bird, "Jesus and the Gentiles after Jeremias: Patterns and Prospects," *CurBR* 4 (2005): 83–108. See the critique of Jeremias by Dieter Zeller in George R. Beasley-Murray, *Jesus and the Kingdom of God* (Grand Rapids, MI: Eerdmans, 1986), 170–72. See also David J. Downs, *The Offering of the Gentiles: Paul's Collection for Jerusalem in its Chronological, Cultural, and Cultic Contexts*, WUNT Reihe 2/248 (Tübingen: Mohr Siebeck, 2008), 3 and n. 9.

43 Bird, "Jesus and the Gentiles after Jeremias," 97.

and disagreement among Jews, "more commonly the expectation was for the Gentiles to come in pilgrimage to Zion to pay tribute or to worship God there."[44] "This affords a positive estimation of the Gentiles by Jesus and posits a qualified continuity between the pre- and post-Easter mission."[45]

The coming of Jesus the Messiah, presented by Jesus himself as a banquet of happiness (Matt 9:15 par.), thus marks the beginning of the fulfillment of the promises. Sending the Twelve to all the nations after his resurrection, Jesus will make possible that eschatological pilgrimage of all people to the new temple, his resurrected body (John 2:21). Let us note, however, how in this situation the chosen people remain, personified in the patriarchs.[46] The great warning hanging over Jesus' adversaries is that they might not eschatologically participate in the destiny reserved for Israel. This destiny will remain through its best representatives, and the gentiles, thanks to the gospel, will have been incorporated into it.

44 James D. G. Dunn, *Jesus Remembered*, Christianity in the Making 1 (Grand Rapids, MI: Eerdmans, 2003), 394. "That Jesus may have shared this hope is suggested by a number of episodes and passages" (Dunn, 538).

45 Bird, "Jesus and the Gentiles after Jeremias," 97.

46 The letter to the Hebrews affirms Levi, Abraham's great-grandson, was already present in Abraham (Heb 7:9–10). The sons are already in the father.

CHAPTER THREE

The Testimony of
the Synoptic Gospels (I):
Mark and Matthew

n the previous chapter we saw some of the fundamental elements of
Jesus' mission, to which the evangelists testify, which show how it is constitutively open to "the nations." Now we will begin an in-depth study
of the different testimonies of the Synoptic Gospels. Despite the peculiari-
ties of each approach, we will be able to appreciate a notable underlying
homogeneity.

A. MARK

Our tour through the Second Gospel will be brief but quite rich, since
we will look closely at some passages that witness to Jesus' consciousness of
the universality of his mission. First (1), we will get oriented with the general
outline of the Gospel; then (2), we will see how a singular exorcism anticipates the salvation offered to the nations. Next (3), we will focus on how the
nations are singularly mentioned in some relevant sayings of Jesus; finally
(4), it will also be fitting to address the Risen Jesus' missionary command
in the *canonical appendix*. The fact that all these passages also appear substantially in Matthew, Luke, or both shows that it is fitting to address Mark's
testimony first.

A.1. The Faith of the Gentiles in Mark's Narrative

The importance, for the whole of the Gospel, of the Roman centurion's declaration after Jesus' death is commonly recognized: "Truly this man was the son of God" (Mark 15:39).[1] In it we see the final point of a journey that begins in Mark 1:1, with a clear example of *inclusio* ("son of God").[2] The theological climax of the Gospel, the most profound confession of Jesus' identity, is therefore treated in the paradoxical context of his death on the cross. And it is from the mouth of a pagan, who thus gives an unexpected fulfillment to Israel's Scriptures. Regarding this subject, Joel Marcus luminously writes the following:

> By his recognition of this profound Christological paradox, the centurion, an "alien from the commonwealth of Israel," a "stranger to the covenants of promise" (cf. Eph 2:12), a pagan from a distant land, becomes the first human in the gospel to grasp the height and depth of Jesus' identity. In so doing, he unwittingly fulfills the triumphant ending of the psalm whose searing words have punctuated the Markan death scene (cf. 15:24, 29–32, 34): "All the ends of the earth shall remember and turn to the LORD; and all the families of the nations shall worship before him. For dominion belongs to the LORD, and he rules over the nations." (Ps 22:27–28)[3]

The confession of Christological faith by a gentile is, then, the culminating moment of the Gospel narration. We shall see some outstanding moments that prepare for this climax.

A.2. Jesus' Activity among the Pagans

In the final parts of the Gospel—during Jesus' activity in Jerusalem—he will refer positively to the divine project of the salvation of all human beings. This project, however, was already anticipated during his ministry in Galilee through his miracles. Though they were ordinarily directed to the people of

---

1 "The Evangelist . . . regards it as of the highest significance." Vincent Taylor, *The Gospel According to St. Mark*, 2nd ed. (London: McMillan, 1966), 598. Cf. Matt 27:54 and Luke 23:47.

2 Joachim Gnilka, *Das Evangelium nach Markus I-II*, 3rd ed., EKKNT II/1 (Zurich: Benziger; Neukirchen: Neukirchener, 1989), 1:26.

3 Joel Marcus, *Mark: A New Translation with Introduction and Commentary*, AB 27–27A (New Haven: Yale University Press, 2000–2009), 2:1068.

Israel, he transcends these limits on two occasions in order to penetrate the land of the pagans.[4]

The first of these occasions is a striking exorcism (Mark 5:1–20).[5] After calming the storm, Jesus arrives at the other side of the sea, "the country of the Gerasenes" (Mark 5:1); this is the area of the Decapolis, on the eastern shore of the Sea of Galilee.[6] Upon disembarking, he meets a demoniac, possessed by a "legion" (5:9) of impure spirits. Even though other Jews were also living in the Decapolis, its population was basically pagan, so that "the possessed man would probably be understood by Mark's readers as a Gentile";[7] the episode therefore constitutes Jesus' first mission into gentile lands in Mark's Gospel.[8] By the power of his word, Jesus will liberate this man from diabolical possession, restoring him to human dignity; he will thus become a preacher of the gospel among the gentiles (5:20). For the moment his ministry to non-Jews will be limited to this intervention; therefore, the man previously possessed by the "legion" of demons will be the first pagan to benefit from Jesus' messianic activity. Jesus will, however, go beyond Israel's limits again to return to gentile territory (the region of Tyre and Sidon: 7:24, 31), where he will enact three important signs: another exorcism (the

4 Jesus was probably already famous among them. One must not forget that according to Mark 3:8, among the multitudes that come to Jesus there are also people "from . . . Idumea and from beyond the Jordan and from about Tyre and Sidon" (Mark 3:8).

5 Cf. Matt 8:28–34 // Luke 8:26–39.

6 The Bible mentions the Decapolis only three times: Matt 4:25; Mark 5:20; 7:31. Gerasa (in Mark's version according to the majority of manuscripts) as well as Gadara and Gergesa (names also found in the manuscript tradition, the last of which is decidedly maintained by Origen) belong to this region. Textual criticism of Mark inclines one to read "Gerasenes," as in Luke, but not in Matthew (which reads "Gadarenes"); see Elisa Estévez López, "El endemoniado de Gerasa: estudio histórico-crítico," in Los milagros de Jesús: Perspectivas metodológicas plurales, ed. Rafael Aguirre Monasterio, ABE 39 (Estella, Spain: Verbo Divino, 2002), 59–62. On the other hand, Joachim Gnilka believes that the original version would have read as "Gergesenes" (Gergesa is the only one of the three cities that borders the Sea of Galilee); a later copyist of Mark would be responsible for substituting Gergesa with Gerasa. Gnilka, Markus, 1:202.

7 Marcus, Mark, 1:342.

8 Luis Manuel Romero Sánchez, La eficacia liberadora de la Palabra de Jesús. La intención pragmática de Mc 5,1–20 en su contexto lingüístico y situacional, ABE 49 (Estella, Spain: Verbo Divino, 2009), 101. Other characteristics of the story point in this direction; cf. Klemens Stock, Marco: Commento contestuale al secondo Vangelo, BibPr 47 (Rome: Edizioni ADP, 2003), 89; Gnilka, Markus, 1:203–4. Gnilka particularly highlights Isaiah 65:1–7, which speaks of the impious and the idolaters.

Syrophoenician woman's daughter), the healing of the deaf-mute, and the second multiplication of the loaves (Mark 7:24–8:10).[9] The last miracle allows us to see how Jesus' ministry begins to fulfill the eschatological banquet for all people (cf. Isa 25:6–8). All of this shows that already during his earthly ministry, Jesus not only manifests his power in Israel, but he also brings salvation to the pagans.[10] These episodes are thus the first fruits of the universal preaching that Jesus will commend to his followers.

A.3. The Nations in the Gospel of Mark

We will now focus on the Gospel passages in which Jesus mentions "the nations" (*ta ethnē*). In three of the five verses in which the word occurs, *the nations* appear as forces that are violent or hostile towards the gospel (Mark 10:33, 42; 13:8). There are, however, two moments in which they appear in a positive light:

1. "And he taught, and said to them, 'Is it not written, *My house shall be called a house of prayer for all the nations?* But you have made it a *den of robbers*'" (Mark 11:17).

   According to the three Synoptic Gospels, Jesus cites Isaiah 56:7 when he purifies the temple: "My house shall be called a house of prayer"; but only Mark adds the final part of the verse in Isaiah ("for all the nations"[11]), thus making these words the center of a double citation of Scripture (Isa 56:7 and Jer 7:11), which forms an antithetical parallelism.[12] In this way Jesus evokes the universality that characterizes the final section of the book of Isaiah: the temple of Jerusalem has a universal vocation.[13] Fol-

---

9 The section, which is absent from Luke, has its parallel in Matthew 15:21–39.

10 Stock, *Marco*, 89.

11 This is how it is translated in the Septuagint. The Hebrew text says, "for all the peoples."

12 Lorenzo Gasparro, *Simbolo e narrazione in Marco: La dimensione simbolica del secondo Vangelo alla luce della pericope del fico di Mc 11,12–25*, AnBib 198 (Rome: Gregorian & Biblical Press, 2012), 428. Cf. Giancarlo Biguzzi, *"Io distruggerò questo tempio": Il tempio e il giudaismo nel vangelo di Marco*, 2nd ed., Percorsi culturali (Rome: Urbaniana University Press, 2008), 41–42.

13 There is thus a difference from the first book of Maccabees, in which the priests—evoking Isaiah 56:7—limit the temple's function solely to Israel: "You chose this house to be called by your name, and to be for your people a place of prayer and supplication" (1 Macc 7:37). Cf. Marcus, *Mark*, 2:783.

lowing Isaiah (cf. Mark 1:2), Mark thus expresses the original significance of the temple as Scripture testifies to it, for its openness to non-Jews was already present in Solomon's dedicatory prayer (1 Kgs 8:41–43).[14]

With his prophetic gesture, Jesus vindicates the purpose of the temple willed by God[15]—a purpose obscured by the activities carried out in it.[16] He thus assumes a universalist perspective that is in clear contrast with the conception (widespread in late Judaism) that the Messiah's eschatological victory over the nations would involve the liberation of the temple from the impure presence of the gentiles.[17] Jesus, contrary to the latter idea, liberates the temple from the merchants, fulfilling the prophecy that is at the end of the book of Zechariah (Zech 14:21); however, he also proclaims its original openness to the nations (Isaiah). Jesus' action is charged with even greater significance if we keep in mind that, in all probability, the money-changing and merchant tables were installed in the Court of the Gentiles, thus making the gentiles' prayer to the God of Israel more difficult.[18]

> In light of the two citations, the "thievery" denounced by Jesus does not refer as much to the iniquity of the commerce . . . as to [the iniquity of] having stolen from the Gentiles the place of prayer designated for them. The question of profanation is not about the pure and the impure, but rather it consists in an abusive change to the original destiny of the sanctuary in the divine project.[19]

---

14 See Steve Moyise, "Is Mark's Opening Quotation the Key to his Use of Scripture?," *IBS* 20 (1998): 157.

15 The double biblical citation connects this prophetic action of Jesus to the will of God: Gasparro, *Simbolo e narrazione*, 427.

16 "The house of prayer for all peoples and the den of thieves are in antithetical parallelism. They contrast the finality assigned by God with human failure." Gnilka, *Markus*, 2:129.

17 This conviction, echoing Ezek 44:5–9, is clearly manifested in a Qumran document that interprets 2 Samuel 7:10 as a reference to the temple: "This (refers to) the house into which shall never enter . . . either the Ammonite, or the Moabite, or the Bastard, or the foreigner, or the proselyte, never, because there [he will reveal] to the holy ones" (4Qflor 1, 3–4). Quoted in Florentino García Martínez, *The Dead Sea Scrolls Translated: The Qumran Texts in English*, 2nd ed. (Leiden: Brill, 1994), 136. For other testimonies, see Marcus, *Mark*, 2:792–93.

18 Cf. Marcus, *Mark*, 2:793.

19 Gasparro, *Simbolo e narrazione*, 430.

Let us note, finally, the importance that the evangelist attributes to these words of Jesus, which are presented as instruction by the Teacher (verb: *didaskō*).[20]

Later Jesus will prophesy the destruction of this temple (Mark 13:1–2); he will thus act as a new Jeremiah (cf. Jer 7:1–15).[21] The universal vocation that belonged to the "house of prayer" will have to be realized in a new form.

2. "But take heed to yourselves; for they will deliver you up to councils; and you will be beaten in synagogues; and you will stand before governors and kings for my sake, to bear testimony before them. And the gospel must first be preached to all nations" (Mark 13:9–10).

While instructing his disciples about the tests that they will endure in the future, Jesus reveals a necessity: it is necessary ("theologically" necessary, Greek: *dei* [God's will]) that the gospel be proclaimed to all the nations. We thus understand the novelty that Jesus introduces: the nations will not be the ones traveling to Jerusalem, but rather the gospel, incarnated in the renewed people of Israel, will be the one traveling to the nations.

We discover the same perspective in another passage of the Gospel, which pertains to the story of the Passion: the anointing of Jesus in Bethany will form part of this gospel that is universally proclaimed. In this way the meaning of the anointing extends beyond prophesying his burial; it also contains a message of life:[22] "And truly, I say to you, wherever the gospel is preached in the whole world, what she has done will be told in memory of her" (Mark 14:9).

"What the woman of Bethany carried out will be an integral part of this announcement. The reason is evident. Without the woman perceiving it, her prophetic action was indissolubly united to Jesus' death, which, together with his resurrection, would form the nucleus, the center, of

20 "And he *taught*, and said to them" (Mark 11:17). In the parallel passages of Matthew and Luke the verb is absent. See in this regard Biguzzi, "*Io distruggerò questo tempio*," 41.

21 Let us remember that Jesus also alludes to Jeremiah 7:11 in Mark 11:17.

22 Cf. Stock, *Marco*, 292.

the preached gospel."[23] This episode will therefore achieve universal dissemination.

In sum, we see how the Second Gospel presents the gentiles, in light of the great prophecies of the Old Testament, as those to whom the Jesus' gospel is addressed. The second conclusion of Mark confirms this.

A.4. The Final Commandment (Canonical Appendix)

The final commandment of the resurrected Christ belongs to the *canonical appendix* of Mark, but it expresses the fulfillment of Jesus' prophecies about the preaching of the gospel to the nations.[24] The passage (Mark 16:15–18) has its parallel in the conclusion of the First Gospel (Matt 28:18–20), but it presents a distinct terminology: "And he said to them, 'Go into all the world and preach the gospel to the whole creation'" (Mark 16:15).

Jesus' last words use the terminology found in Mark 13:10 and 14:9 once more ("preach the gospel"), with the same universal perspective. What was earlier a prophecy of the future is now the work of the present. The range of addressees is maximal, as highlighted by the insistence on totality: "*all* the world" (*eis ton kosmon hapanta*), "the *whole* creation" (*pasē tē ktísei*). The evangelist's report culminates in his confirmation of the fulfillment of this commandment: "And they went forth and preached everywhere, while the Lord worked with them and confirmed the message by the signs that attended it. Amen" (Mark 16:20).

Even though these words do not belong to the original plan of the Gospel, they are consonant with the other passages that we have surveyed. With its characteristic sobriety, the canonical Gospel of Mark therefore reflects the universal call of the gospel of Jesus Christ, which thus fulfills the universality of the "gospel of the kingdom" announced in the prophetic writings.

---

23 Francisco Pérez Herrero, *Pasión y Pascua de Jesús según san Marcos*, PFTNE.B 67 (Burgos: Facultad de Teología del Norte de España, 2001), 68.

24 Cf. William R. Farmer, *The Last Twelve Verses of Mark*, SNTSMS 25 (Cambridge: Cambridge University Press, 1974).

A.5. Conclusion: The Bread for the Children

"The time is fulfilled": these inaugural words of Jesus (Mark 1:15) mark the beginning of the definitive revelation of God's salvific plan—a plan that extends to all nations. This does not, however, minimize the relevance of the chosen people. To the Syrophoenician woman, Jesus manifests his desire to "let the children first be fed" (or "satiated"; 7:27). Jesus has come to "satiate" Israel's hunger, to fulfill completely the hopes of his people.[25] This must come to pass "first," and the salvation for the nations will come as an overflowing from that satiety ("the children's crumbs").[26] The abundance of that salvation that Jesus brings to Israel will overflow in favor of all humanity.

B. MATTHEW

In the Christian canon, the first Gospel is that of Matthew. Of apostolic origin (according to the traditional attribution), this Gospel has played and continues to play a very relevant role in the life and teaching of the Church. How is the universal openness of Jesus' mission manifested in it?

B.1. The Gospel of Matthew and the "Nations"

Jesus prophesies twice in Matthew the universal spreading of the good news (Matt 24:14 and 26:13; these are in parallel with Mark 13:10 and 14:9, commented on above). It is valuable to examine two terms, *gospel* and *nations*, to understand the vision that the Gospel proposes about this diffusion.

a) "Gospel" in Matthew

We previously examined the biblical background of the term "gospel" (*euangelion*), which in Matthew appears only four times: in the two summaries of Jesus' activity in Galilee (Matt 4:23 and 9:35), and in the two verses just mentioned (Matt 24:14 and 26:13: "this gospel"). The term is always either the

---

25 The verb *chortazō* will only appear again in the two accounts of Jesus multiplying the loaves, with markedly symbolic significance (Mark 6:42; 8:4, 8).

26 "The word *prōton*, and the thought behind it, are similar to those of Paul in Rom 1:16 and Rom 11: Jesus came for the Jews first, but also for the Gentiles." Marcus, *Mark*, 1:463.

subject or object of the verb *to preach* or *to proclaim* (which occurs 9 times in Matthew).[27] The word *gospel* at times refers to the kingdom of heaven—that is, the "gospel of the kingdom" (4:23; 9:35; 24:14). In 4:23, this expression adds specification to the initial preaching of Jesus ("From that time Jesus began to preach [*kēryssō*], saying, 'Repent, for the kingdom of heaven is at hand'": 4:17), which gives us an idea of its centrality in Jesus' ministry.

The verb "announce good news" (*euangelizomai*) only appears once in Matthew, in an allusion to Isaiah 61:1: "Go and tell John what you hear and see: the blind receive their sight and the lame walk, lepers are cleansed and the deaf hear, and the dead are raised up, and the poor have good news preached to them [*ptōchoi euangelizontai*]" (Matt 11:4–5).

Jesus' compact declaration culminates in this verb; in light of Matthew 11:5, therefore, the substantive *euangelion*, in the various places where it appears, is situated in the wake of the *euangelizomai* of the Old Testament. This confirms what we deduced from the combination of "gospel" and "kingdom of God."

By virtue of its biblical background, the gospel of the kingdom (Matt 4:23) therefore appears as the eschatological fulfillment of the prophetic Scriptures, which will mark the beginning of the mission among the gentiles. It is from this perspective that we must understand the "gospel" of Jesus; the term "nation" in Matthew also points in this direction.

b) The "Nations" in Matthew

Ethnos (nation), referring to the peoples who are pagan and thereby differentiated from the Jewish People, has diverse connotations in Matthew. In the didactic sections it has a negative sense, in continuity with the Jewish usage:[28] "the nations" are excessively occupied with temporal questions (Matt 6:32); the princes of the nations rule tyrannically (20:25). The nations will kill Jesus (20:19); the disciples will suffer in giving testimony before the nations (10:18); all the nations, mutually opposing each other (24:7), will hate the disciples because of the name of Jesus (24:9). This pejorative sense also characterizes the adjective *ethnikos* (gentile: 5:47; 6:7; 18:17), as revealed by the

---

27 *Kēryssō:* Matt 3:1; 4:17, 23; 9:35; 10:7, 27; 11:1; 24:14; 26:13.

28 Nikolaus Walter, "ἔθνος," *EDNT* 1:382.

respective contexts and the terms with which it appears to be related (tax collectors: 5:46 and 18:17; hypocrites: 6:5).

Nevertheless, it would be erroneous to deduce from these texts a unilaterally negative vision of the nations in Matthew. In fact, in the *infancy narrative*, the episode of the Magi shows us some pagans who, in relation to the prophecy of Balaam (Num 24:17), come to adore the king of the Jews (Matt 2:1–12). And near the end of the Gospel, we are taught that in the final judgment "all the nations" will be gathered together before the Son of Man (25:32), and among all of them—independent of their condition as gentiles—there will be just and unjust people (25:46).

These passages relate to a second group of Matthean passages, in which the "nations" appear under a different light. We encounter the term *ethnos* for the first time in a "fulfillment citation," the fifth one of this Gospel. The "Galilee of the Gentiles" (Matt 4:15; Isa 8:23), a designation that for Matthew does not pretend to be historical but theological, is the setting of the apparition of the "great light" (Matt 4:16; Isa 9:1), that is to say, of the preaching of Jesus.[29] However we interpret the expression, the mention of the nations draws our attention to this theme.[30] The evangelist is particularly interested in relating the first proclamation of the gospel of the kingdom to the nations (cf. 4:17).[31] In this way, the *revelation* to the "Galilee of the Gentiles" appears as a prefiguration of the announcement of salvation to all the nations.[32] Something similar occurs with the seventh fulfillment citation, the longest of this Gospel and also of Isaiah (Matt 12:18–21; Isa 42:1–4); the presentation of Jesus as the meek and humble Servant (cf. Matt 11:29) is framed by the term "nations," in the plural. In Matthew 12:18 (=Isa 42:1) we are taught that the Servant "shall

29 "With this OT designation Matthew wants on a secondary level to point ahead to what Jesus' sending has begun in the history of salvation: the movement of salvation to the Gentiles." Ulrich Luz, *Matthew 1–7. A Commentary*, Hermeneia (Minneapolis: Fortress, 2007), 158.

30 "*Galilee of the nations* would then designate Galilee as a territory in which pagans reside, or which is open to and turned towards the nations." Jean Miler, *Les citations d'accomplissement dans l'Évangile de Matthieu. Quand Dieu se rend présent en toute humanité*, AnBib 140 (Rome: Pontificio Istituto Biblico, 1999), 84.

31 "Jesus is the eschatological light for Israel in Galilee as well as for the nations." Guido Tisera, *Universalism According to the Gospel of Matthew*, EHS.T 482 (Frankfurt am Main: Peter Lang, 1993), 98.

32 Miler, *Citations*, 102.

proclaim justice to the Gentiles." And the citation concludes, "and in his name will the Gentiles hope" (Matt 12:21: Isa 42:4b LXX).[33]

We see, then, that the presentation of the nations in a positive light occurs in certain passages referring to prophetic Scripture, and more concretely to Isaiah. The evangelist, from the beginning and with the support of the great prophet, presents Jesus' public ministry as having a universal horizon. Let us note that this initial presentation of the nations (Matt 4:15) is in conformity with the great missionary commandment that closes the Gospel: "Go therefore and make disciples of all nations" (28:19).[34] He whose ministry signified the dawn of salvation for the nations (4:15) commends a universal mission to the Eleven after his resurrection.

c) Conclusion: The Nations, at the Center of the Gospel

The gospel of the kingdom will be proclaimed throughout the whole world as testimony for all the nations (Matt 24:14). What we have indicated about the universal openness of Jesus' ministry shows us that this affirmation does not rest on an isolated passage of the Gospel, but on the contrary, it condenses its central message. Both the study of *euangelion* and that of *ethnos* have shown the roots of this fact in prophetic Scripture, which Jesus fulfills.

B.2. Mission to the Nations and Mission to Israel in Matthew

In the First Gospel, the gentiles are never presented as an example of piety or morality; as we have seen, their presence in Jesus' teaching bears a predominantly negative connotation. The pagans limit their gestures of affection to their kin, closing themselves off to the stranger (Matt 5:47); they multiply "empty words" in their prayer (6:7); they toil for worldly things (6:32); they are strangers to the community of the disciples (18:17). This helps us to understand that the gentiles' religiosity is evaluated negatively by Jesus: being ignorant of the true face of God, it inspires erroneous behavior.

---

33 "With authority the Servant-Son announces the *krisis* unto the ends of the earth." Miler, *Citations*, 148.

34 See Richard Beaton, *Isaiah's Christ in Matthew's Gospel*, SNTSMS 123 (Cambridge: Cambridge University Press, 2002), 110.

This negative evaluation coincides with some *logia* of Jesus in Matthew's Gospel that seem to contradict universal openness. On the one hand, the gentiles are excluded from Jesus' ministry and from that of his disciples ("Go nowhere among the Gentiles . . . but go rather to the lost sheep of the house of Israel": 10:5b–6; "I was sent only to the lost sheep of the house of Israel": 15:24). On the other hand, the conclusion of the Gospel affirms this mission as an indispensable obligation ("make disciples of all nations": 28:19; cf. 24:14). Do we have an unresolvable contradiction?

a) The Nations and the Twelve

We must focus first of all on the context of Jesus' declaration at the beginning of his missionary discourse (10:5b–6).[35] The discourse immediately follows the enumeration of the Twelve (10:2–4), whom Jesus has just constituted as a group and who are thus now named for the first time in the Gospel ("his twelve disciples": 10:1; "the twelve apostles": 10:2). "These twelve Jesus sent out" (10:5a): the mission that is restricted to Israel has a close relationship, therefore, with the constitution of the Twelve.[36] It is a moment of fundamental importance for understanding Jesus' ministry, but its connotations—which are evident for a Jew familiar with Scripture—remain veiled by the sobriety of the narration. It will, however, become transparent in an instruction on the way to Jerusalem, with which we are already familiar (19:28). Let us recall what we have seen in the previous chapter about the election of the Twelve.

Hence it is coherent, from the narrative standpoint, that the inaugural mission of the Twelve is circumscribed to Israel (Matt 10:5); the name and structure that Jesus wanted to confer on the group of disciples (Matt 10:1–4) makes intrinsic reference to the chosen people. As Nikolaus Walter puts it, "Matthew is thereby describing an epoch which lies in the past."[37]

---

35 Cf. Luis Sánchez-Navarro, "La Escritura para las naciones: Acerca del universalismo en Mateo," *ScrTh* 40 (2008): 525–41.

36 The "missionary discourse" (10:5–11:1) closes with an expression ("his twelve disciples": 11:1) that forms an *inclusio* with 10:1. The Twelve are again mentioned as such in 20:17; 26:14, 20, 47. After the resurrection they will be "the eleven disciples" (28:16).

37 Walter, "ἔθνος," 383.

However, we no longer have to understand the people of Israel as the exclusive and ultimate recipient of God's salvation. Now it is the eschatologically renewed people that, according to the promises of Scripture, will allow all of humanity to access the salvation offered by the God of Israel, in such a way that Israel's mission is necessary for the gospel to be brought to "all the nations."[38]

b) The Mission to the Nations in Matthew: Fulfillment of Scripture

Matthew especially emphasizes the universal mission; in order to understand it, we must return to the double biblical reference. The initial presentation of the nations is positive: the "Galilee of the Gentiles" represents the scenario of Jesus' manifestation (Matt 4:15). And within the Gospel, Jesus' ministry is insistently referred to the nations with a fulfillment citation of recognizable importance (12:18–21; Isa 42:1–4). It is therefore Isaiah, mentioned twice by name (Matt 4:14; 12:17), who spoke of the universal mission of this Servant. Jesus does nothing but fulfill that hope.

The Twelve must limit their missionary activity to Israel, because Jesus has come to the "lost sheep of the house of Israel." He has come to search for them so that none of "these little ones should perish" (18:12–14) and does so in order to reintegrate them into Israel, the reconstituted Israel whose fundamental structure is made up of the Twelve. It is through this renewed Israel that the universal mission of the mysterious Servant of the Lord can be realized. Therefore, once Jesus has renewed the covenant through his death (cf. "my blood of the covenant": 26:28)—a death whose saving fruit has vast dimensions ("for many": 26:28) and through which he has reunited the dispersed sheep[39]—he can commend to the Eleven the great mission for which he has called them: making disciples of all nations (28:19).

---

38 "Israel's restoration means that the salvation of the gentile nations is at hand. Jesus' death and resurrection bring about an eschatological era of salvation for all." Tisera, *Universalism*, 332–33.

39 "You will all fall away because of me this night; for it is written, 'I will strike the shepherd, and the sheep of the flock will be scattered.' But after I am raised up, I will go before you to Galilee" (Matt 26:31–32). Cf. 28:10.

This perspective stands out at other moments in the Gospel; we have seen in the episode of the Magi how—in contrast with the Jews of Jerusalem—some gentiles coming from the Orient adore Jesus (Matt 2:1–12). They adore, however, the one whom they recognize as the "king of the Jews" (2:2); hence they look for salvation in the eschatological fullness of Israel, just as revealed by the allusion to Isaiah 60:6 in Matthew 2:11.[40] Already from the narration of Jesus' infancy, he is presented as the bearer of salvation for the gentiles, but he does so in his capacity as king of Israel, and not by denying that condition. This perspective also appears in the general framework of the Gospel, as we shall appreciate in the following part.

c) Conclusion

According to Matthew, Jesus' messianic mission to Israel implies Israel's openness to the nations; the universal mission can only be realized—according to Scripture—in this context of eschatological fulfillment. Therefore, no contradiction exists: both missions need each other. It is necessary for the Twelve to go only to the lost sheep of the house of Israel (10:6) so that they can be sent to all the nations (28:19). One last observation should be made: the *ekklēsia* of Jesus (cf. 16:18), structured around the Twelve (Eleven), is not understood in itself as the true Israel in opposition to the Jewish People—which, consequently, would have to be deprived of that title. The Church is the "renewed Israel," and by the fact of being so, she is open to the nations.[41] She does not, however, supplant or invalidate the historical Israel, but with her very existence she constantly invites these chosen people to participate in Jesus through that renovation.

---

40 "A multitude of camels shall cover you, the young camels of Midian and Ephah; all those from Sheba shall come. They shall bring gold and frankincense and shall proclaim the praise of the LORD" (Isa 60:6).

41 She is the new wineskin (Matt 9:17), which is capable of receiving the new wine of the kingdom of the Father (26:29); in both passages the adjective *kainos* (new) appears (cf. Jer 31:31 and Luke 22:20: "new covenant").

B.3. The Framework of the Gospel (Matt 1:1; 28:19)

We discover the "Judeo-Christian" character of the First Gospel in its very opening (the genealogy of Jesus): it begins with Abraham and Isaac (Matt 1:2) and is thus limited to those genealogical connections that belong to the Israelite lineage from the patriarchs. The perspective is particular, oriented towards Israel; Jesus is shown as the son of the promise made to David and Abraham (1:1).

We must, however, clarify this impression immediately. From the very outset there is a surprising fact: none of the four women mentioned in this genealogy (Tamar, Rahab, Ruth, or the wife of Uriah) is Jewish; "so through them the world of the Gentiles enters the genealogy of Jesus—his mission to Jews *and* Gentiles is made manifest."[42] This is in conformity with the beginning itself of this genealogy, where it is affirmed that Jesus is the "son of Abraham" (1:1). It is the only time that this expression appears in the New Testament in reference to Jesus; it is different from the phrase that accompanies it: "son of David," a title that frequently refers to him in Matthew and in the other Synoptic Gospels.[43] But "son of Abraham" is also distinct from "son of David" in that this latter expression makes a direct reference to the kingdom of Israel. On the contrary, the figure of Abraham has in itself a wider dimension, not only because Abraham is also the father of Ishmael (and therefore of other peoples outside of Israel),[44] but above all because of the promise with which we are already familiar, and that accompanies Abraham from the beginning of his history: "and by you all the families [*pasai hai phylai*: LXX] of the earth shall bless themselves" (Gen 12:3); "seeing that Abraham shall become a great and mighty nation, and all the nations [*panta ta ethnē*: LXX] of the earth shall bless themselves by him?" (Gen 18:18); "and by your descendants shall all the nations [*panta ta ethnē*: LXX] of the earth bless themselves, because you have obeyed my voice" (Gen 22:18).

---

42 Joseph Ratzinger (Benedict XVI), *Jesus of Nazareth: The Infancy Narratives*, trans. Philip J. Whitmore (New York: Image, 2012), 7.

43 In Luke 19:9 "son of Abraham" is predicated of Zacchaeus; cf. also Luke 13:16: "daughter of Abraham." "Son of David": Matt 9:27; 12:23; 15:22; 20:30–31; 21:9, 15; cf. 22:42, 45. See also Mark 10:47–48; 12:35; 18:38–39; 20:41, 44; Rom 1:3. In Matt 1:20 the angel addresses Joseph as "Joseph, son of David."

44 For his part, Ishmael will have twelve sons, who will be fathers of many other nations (Gen 25:12–16).

Through Abraham must come the blessing for "all the nations of the earth"; he is therefore a figure that is at once particular (in his special reference to Israel) and universal. The mention of him in Matthew 1:1–2 unites both dimensions; this impression is confirmed by Matthew 8:11, which affirms that—in contrast to the "sons of the kingdom" (8:12)—many coming from the East (let us recall the Magi) and from the West will "sit at table with Abraham, Isaac, and Jacob in the kingdom of heaven." The gentiles are called to be integrated into the eschatological banquet of Israel, the lineage of Abraham. And they will accomplish it through Jesus. Abraham is quintessentially the bearer of the promise, in such a way that Matthew, by calling Jesus the "son of Abraham" (in an approach surprisingly close to the one Paul develops in Galatians 3:16–29), presents him as the one who will fulfill that promise.

The biblical background thus makes it possible for us to uncover a thematic parallel between the beginning of the Gospel ("son of Abraham" [*huios Abraam*]: 1:1) and its conclusion ("all the nations" [*panta ta ethne*]: 28:19). The opening of the Gospel hints at the universal mission of the resurrected Christ, intimately linked to the sending of Israel.

> From the beginning of the genealogy, then, the focus is already on the end of the gospel, when the Risen Lord says to his disciples: "Make disciples of all nations" (Matt 28:19). In the particular history revealed by the genealogy, this movement towards the whole is present from the beginning; the universality of Jesus' mission is already contained within its origin.[45]

B.4. The Nations and the "Sons of the Kingdom"

A passage to which I have just alluded, however, raises doubts about the final destiny of the people of Israel. On the occasion of healing the centurion's servant, Jesus affirms that—in contrast to "many" gentiles—"the sons of the kingdom will be thrown into the outer darkness; there men will weep and gnash their teeth" (Matt 8:12).[46] Without doubt in this context the expres-

45 Ratzinger, *Infancy Narratives*, 5.

46 See the text of Matthew and its parallel in Luke (Luke 13:28b). Davies and Allison maintain that those who come "from the east and the west" (8:11) are not Gentiles, but Jews of the diaspora. William D. Davies and Dale C. Allison, Jr., *The Gospel According to Saint Matthew*, 3 vols., ICC (Edinburgh: T&T Clark, 1988–97), 2:26–29. But the context in which this word of

sion "the sons of the kingdom" refers to the Jewish People.[47] A similar outlook dominates the conclusion of the parable of the homicidal vineyard workers, in which Jesus now directly addresses his interlocutors (chief priests and Pharisees: 21:45): "Therefore I tell you the kingdom of God will be taken away from you and given to a nation producing the fruits of it" (Matt 21:43).[48] It is inevitable that one will ask, Does this imply a rupture with Israel?[49] Does Jesus consider it impossible for God to keep his covenant with his people? Does this contradict God's fidelity, revealed in his son Jesus?

Let us note first of all that both of Jesus' sayings appear in contexts from which they cannot be detached. In Matthew 8–9, Jesus preaches and heals in Israel, so that the curing of the centurion's servant in Capernaum is "an initial flash of lightning" of the destiny of the pagans.[50] This event is framed by other healings, in which the faith of his beneficiaries, all of them belonging to the chosen people, is also emphasized (cf. 9:2, 22, 28–29). On the other hand, we cannot lose sight of what W. D. Davies and D. C. Allison affirm about the "literary genre" of this word of Jesus, namely, that it is hyperbole, a form of expression that evokes the prophetic genre.[51]

In effect, prophetic literature often combines seemingly incompatible affirmations (e.g., threat and promise) in the same book; numerous examples exist. We thus see how Isaiah announces the destruction of the vine of

---

Jesus appears (where the centurion, certainly a pagan, has his faith contrasted by Jesus with that of Israel: 8:5-10) suggests that those "many" likely refer to the gentiles; see Richard T. France, *The Gospel of Matthew*, NICNT (Grand Rapids, MI: Eerdmans, 2007), 318. "In its new context, those from the east . . . and west are Gentiles." Ian Boxall, "Matthew," in *JBC XXI*, 1187.

47 In Matthew 13:38, on the contrary, the same expression refers to the Christians. Davies and Allison, *Matthew*, 2:30.

48 The versions of the parable in Mark (12:1-12) and Luke (20:9-19) do not contain an explicit affirmation parallel to this one.

49 Wolfgang Trilling also maintains this in *Das Wahre Israel: Studien zur Theologie des Matthäus-Evangeliums*, 3rd ed. SANT 10 (Munich: Kösel-Verlag, 1964), 88–90, referring to Matt 8:12. Bonnard also seems to understand it this way: "Here [Matt 8:11-12] there is no final 'mercy' as in Rom 9 to 11." Pierre Bonnard, *L'Évangile selon Saint Matthieu*, CNT 1 (Neuchâtel: Delachaux & Niestle, 1970), 116.

50 Ulrich Luz, *Matthew 8-20: A Commentary*, Hermeneia (Minneapolis: Fortress, 2001), 11.

51 "Hyperboles abound in the synoptic tradition, and the searing antithesis in Matt 8.11f., with its seemingly sweeping condemnation of a whole class, is the kind of black and white declaration one hesitates to take at face value. Poetic license must be given its due." Davies and Allison, *Matthew*, 2:31.

Israel (Isa 5:5–7) while shortly afterward announcing the birth of a son who will establish the throne of David, thus demonstrating how the people can, despite its ruin, be restored (Isa 9:1–6).[52] Something similar occurs in the book of Jeremiah: if the words about the temple suggest a definitive destruction of the people (Jer 7:12–15), this impression is corrected by the prophecies of restoration (Jer 23:5–8; 31:31–34). For the rest, the denouncement of the people's sins and the announcement of the ruin that will come to Israel from its sins, in the context of the *rîb*, is a common feature of the prophets.[53] But this ruin is not definitive: "Threats generally form part of the exhortation."[54]

A different case is Matthew 21:43; in a context of controversy, a first reading would suggest a logic of substitution: the people of Israel is substituted by a new people, the Church. But the reality is more complex. The prophetic force of these words of Jesus is undeniable; it is a warning to the chosen people. We are, however, far from a "logic of substitution"; in this regard, Ulrich Luz correctly maintains that "it is not about the Church taking the place of Israel but an appeal to those who thus far did not belong to Israel to bring fruits."[55] This new people is not simply made up of the gentiles in

---

52 In Isaiah, one observes an evolution: its first major part (Isa 1–39) emphasizes Israel's sin, which results in punishment, whereas the second part (Isa 40–55) places more focus on salvation, and sin is only its counterpoint. Finally, the last part (Isa 56–66) announces the restoration of Israel, a "new creation" in which there will be no room for sin. Cf. Santiago Ausín Olmos, "Pecado," in *Diccionario del Profetismo bíblico*, ed. José Luis Barriocanal (Burgos: Monte Carmelo, 2008), 540–41.

53 Regarding the relationship between sin and death in prophetic preaching, see Paul Beauchamp, *Ley, Profetas, Sabios: Lectura sincrónica del Antiguo Testamento* (Madrid: Cristiandad, 1977), 87–89.

54 Jesús M. Asurmendi Ruiz, "Géneros literarios," in *Diccionario del Profetismo bíblico*, ed. José Luis Barriocanal (Burgos: Monte Carmelo, 2008), 320.

55 Ulrich Luz, *Matthew 21–28: A Commentary*, Hermeneia (Minneapolis: Fortress, 2005), 43.

opposition to Israel,[56] even though the term "nation" brings them to mind;[57] rather, it is the community of believers in Jesus, who are Jews and gentiles.[58]

Finally, let us make a hermeneutical observation. The principal interpretive criterion of the Gospel text must always be its *context*: each passage is explained by the totality, and in turn each part enriches and influences the whole.[59] From this perspective an illuminating observation by Isidro Gomá becomes particularly poignant: "It is typical of Jesus' popular style to have a certain 'absolutism' of form in each of his affirmations, which must be harmonized with another complementary affirmation, which is also apparently 'absolute.' Only in the proportional synthesis of both does the Master's thinking appear *complete*."[60] This observation, which the author affirmed about Matthew 7:6, has a validity that fits better still when Jesus adopts the prophetic genre in a polemical context.

B.5. Conclusion: The Gospel of Matthew, Scripture for the Nations

After our tour through the First Gospel, we can speak of Matthew as an evangelist with a clearly universal perspective. But he is not opposed to Hebrew Scripture in this regard; on the contrary, in the proclamation of his gospel, Jesus fulfills that Scripture. It is not adequate to have an approach that obliges us to decide between a mission to Israel and a mission to the nations, emphasizing the apparent contradiction of Matthew 10:5b–6 and 15:24 with 28:19. The first mission necessarily implies the second; not only does it not deny it, but it makes it possible. As Joachim Jeremias says, citing

---

56 This is how it is interpreted by Joachim Jeremias, *The Parables of Jesus*, 2nd ed. (New York: Charles Scribner's Sons, 1972), 77. But in this case one would have expected the plural "nations," in place of the singular "nation" (the only time in the Gospel in which it appears in the singular; Matt 24:7 is no exception). Cf. Isidro Gomá Civit, *El evangelio según San Mateo*, 2 vols. (Madrid: Marova, 1976), 369–70.

57 Tisera, *Universalism*, 233 n. 74: "*Ethnos* is indeterminate but evokes *ethnē* as well."

58 Gomá Civit, *San Mateo*, 2:370; Antonio Rodríguez Carmona, *Evangelio de Mateo*, CBJer 1A (Bilbao: Desclée de Brouwer, 2006), 190.

59 Stock, *Marco*, 12–13.

60 Gomá Civit, *San Mateo*, 1:393–94.

Johannes Munck, "the reason why Jesus came to Israel was precisely because his mission concerned the whole world."[61]

Precisely because the Scriptures are fulfilled in Jesus (cf. Matt 1:23; 5:17; 26:56), his ministry to Israel—having the eschatological character of the "evangelizer" of Deutero-Isaiah (Isa 52:7)—achieves the universal dimension proper to the Servant of the Lord in whose name the nations hope (Matt 12:21; Isa 42:4) and who, moreover, has been constituted as the light of the nations (Isa 42:6; 49:6). The First Gospel thus becomes the fulfillment of the Scripture that makes it universal; it is therefore the gospel in its totality, the Scripture of Israel that opens to the nations.

61 Jeremias, *Jesus' Promise*, 73.

CHAPTER FOUR

The Testimony of the Synoptic Gospels (II): Luke and the Acts of the Apostles

L uke's two-part work is unique. On the one hand, it represents the writing of a single author that is the most extensive in the whole New Testament, constituting more than a quarter part of it.[1] The main originality of his two books, however, lies in the continuity between the life of Jesus (the Gospel) and the life of the community of his disciples (Acts). Other New Testament authors (Paul, John, and Peter) present more than one canonical writing, but only Luke presents his writings as two distinct parts of a single literary-theological project. This fact is related to the theme that concerns us.[2] The second part—the book of Acts—will describe the universal expansion of the Church, but already in the Gospel we find indications of this openness, so that we can consider the universality of salvation to be one of the fundamental theological questions of the entire Lukan work.[3] The theme is related to the continuity of salvation between Israel and the Church, a theme in which Luke manifests a primordial interest.[4]

---

1 In total 2,157 verses (1,151 in Luke and 1,006 in Acts); the New Testament consists of 7,956 verses. The thirteen letters of Paul (not including Hebrews) consist of 2,032 verses.

2 Cf. Stephen G. Wilson, *The Gentiles and the Gentile Mission in Luke-Acts*, SNTSMS 23 (Cambridge: Cambridge University Press, 1973).

3 "A major theological concern of Luke." Robert F. O'Toole, *The Unity of Luke's Theology: An Analysis of Luke-Acts*, GNS 9 (Wilmington, DE: Michael Glazier, 1984), 108; the whole chapter (99–108) is titled "The Universality of Salvation."

4 "Luke's main theological theme is that God who brought salvation to his people in the Old Testament continues to do this, especially through Jesus Christ." O'Toole, *The Unity of Luke's Theology*, 17.

A. THE GOSPEL OF LUKE

Compared to the two preceding Gospels, Luke's Gospel is characterized, among other features, by its almost complete exclusion of Jesus' mission among non-Jews during his public life; in fact, we do not find a parallel to the section in Mark 7:24–8:10 (// Matt 15:21–39), in which Jesus passes to the north and east of Galilee and thus outside of the limits of Israel.[5] But there is no shortage of indications of universal openness, though they are more latent than in Matthew and Mark. In chapter 2, we addressed some characteristics that Luke shares with Matthew and Mark; now we will focus on certain passages that are exclusive to the Third Gospel.

A.1. The Infancy Narrative (Luke 1–2)

In the first chapter is announced the virginal birth of Jesus, Son of the Most High, who will receive "the throne of his father David" and who "will reign over the house of David forever" (Luke 1:31–33). His mission is therefore circumscribed by Israel; in fact, in her song Mary celebrates the help given to "his servant Israel," in fulfillment of the promise made to Abraham (1:54–55). It is the same perspective as the one we discover in the "Benedictus," in which Zechariah comments on the significance of Jesus' birth and John's birth for God's "people" (1:68–79). The Lord the Messiah who is born in the city of David (Bethlehem) is similarly a cause of happiness for "all the people" (2:10–11). Therefore, if the song of the angels invokes peace "on earth . . . among men with whom he is pleased" (2:14), it all seems to indicate that the reference is to the faithful Jews, the "poor of the Lord" ('anawîm). Eight days after Jesus' birth he will be circumcised (2:21), and at 40 days the family will ascend to the temple in order to proceed with the rites of purification "according to the law of Moses" (2:22; cf. Lev 12:2–4) and to present the first-born according to this same law (2:23–24; cf. Exod 13:2, 12). Jesus appears as a true son of Israel, whose mission is aimed at the chosen people.

So confesses Simon, who has been "looking forward to the consolation of Israel" (2:25) and who recognizes the child Jesus as the Messiah of the Lord

---

5 We have an exception: the healing of the Gerasene demoniac (Luke 8:26–39); see in this respect the exposition of Mark 5:1–20.

(2:26–28); also, the aged prophetess Anna sees in this child the arrival of the long-awaited redemption of Jerusalem (2:38). It is interesting, however, to note how Simeon describes this "salvation" of God (2:30): "a light for revelation to the Gentiles, and for glory to your people Israel" (2:32);[6] additionally, God has prepared this salvation "in the presence of all peoples" (2:31).[7] Here, with a typical midrashic technique of interpretation, Isaiah's words about the Servant of the Lord as a "light to the nations" (Isa 42:6; 49:6) are applied to Jesus. The prophetic words of Simeon are the first words that, in this Gospel, manifest a universal dimension of Jesus' mission, even though they are inseparable from his mission in favor of the chosen people: "Jesus' mission will be to become an instrument of salvation for all the peoples, Jews and gentiles alike, and thus to bring the glory of Israel, fulfilling the Jewish expectations."[8] From the beginning of Jesus' earthly history, centered in Israel, there is already a demonstrated openness to all human beings.

A.2. Beginning of the Ministry of Jesus (Luke 3–4)

One can also discern this openness in the preparation for Jesus' mission; the ministry of his precursor will have the effect of "all flesh" (that is, all human beings) seeing "the salvation of God" (Luke 3:6; Isa 40:5), so that the Baptist's activity is oriented to the universal salvation in Jesus Christ.[9] In this way the parallelism between Jesus and his precursor is highlighted: John's ministry is the prelude to the great theme of Luke-Acts, which is the addition of the gentiles along with Israel.[10] After the baptism of Jesus we see

---

6 The Codex Bezae, an important manuscript from the 5th century AD, offers a distinct reading of v. 32; it omits the word *nations*: "a light for revelation and for glory to your people Israel." The perspective is thus distinct in that it is particular and without universal openness.

7 "The expression *pantōn tōn laōn* refers to all peoples, from either pagan nations or the Jewish nation." Andrés García Serrano, *The Presentation in the Temple: The Narrative Function of Lk 2:22–39 in Luke-Acts*, AnBib 197 (Rome: Gregorian & Biblical Press, 2012), 178.

8 García Serrano, *The Presentation in the Temple*, 181.

9 Hady Mahfouz, *La fonction littéraire et théologique de Lc 3,1–20 dans Luc-Actes*, USEK.T 11 (Kaslik: Université Saint-Esprit, 2003), 157. "In Luke 3:6, the evangelist takes up the theme of the universality of salvation, already announced in Luke 1–2 (cf. Luke 2:31–32); he clearly alludes to it with a similar expression, at the end of his work, in Acts 28:28" (Mahfouz, 156).

10 Cf. Bart J. Koet, "Isaiah in Luke-Acts," in *Isaiah in the New Testament*, ed. S. Moyise and M. J. J. Menken, NTSI (London: 2005), 82–83.

his genealogy; in contrast to that of Matthew (which begins with Abraham), Luke presents to us Jesus' family origins in ascending order moving backwards through time, not only back to David (Luke 3:31) and Abraham (3:34), but all the way back to Adam and from him to God (3:38). In this way Jesus is shown in his relationship with the chosen people, but also—and above all—with all of humanity (recall that in Hebrew Adam signifies "man").[11] The evangelist thus demonstrates that Jesus is the son of God, not only by virtue of his virginal conception, but also through his human genealogy; furthermore, in this way he relates to all the other children of Adam at the same time.

On the other hand, the beginning of his public life, with references to the rulers of the empire and of Palestine (Luke 3:1–2; cf. also 2:1–2), situates the event of Jesus in its broader context. Therefore, the framework is not Israel alone but also the known world at that time, under the dominion of Rome; Jesus' history thus enters into relationship with universal history.[12] A final observation: as we have already seen, Jesus' inaugural preaching in the synagogue of Nazareth evokes the activity of Israel's great prophets Elijah and Elisha, but it does so in light of a universal reach that exceeds the limits of the chosen people (the widow in Zarephath of Sidon and the leper Naaman the Syrian; Luke 4:24–27). The allusion of Jesus to the salvation of the non-Jews, which will provoke the homicidal ire of his fellow citizens (4:28–29), is a prelude to the universal reach of the gospel that the Risen Christ will openly affirm.

A.3. THE COMMANDMENT
OF THE RISEN CHRIST (LUKE 24:46–47)

We have to reach the end of the Gospel to see the Risen Christ making explicit the true dimension of his salvation: "Thus it is written, that the Christ should suffer and on the third day rise from the dead, and that repentance

---

11 "Mathew's genealogy is openly 'messianic'…, highlighting Jesus' relation to Israel and its famous forebears, David and Abraham, whereas Luke's genealogy is that of Jesus, the Son of God, with David and Abraham mentioned only as ordinary ancestors in a line going back to the first of human beings, Adam." Joseph A. Fitzmyer, *The Gospel According to Luke*, 2 vols., AB 28–28A (New York: Doubleday, 1981), 1:495.

12 Fitzmyer, *Luke*, 2:1580.

and forgiveness of sins should be preached in his name to all nations, beginning from Jerusalem" (24:46–47). In this last apparition Jesus reiterates the
essential aspects of his instruction to the disciples that were walking to
Emmaus, regarding the theological necessity for the Messiah to suffer in
fulfillment of the Scriptures (24:26–26). Now, however, he adds something
new: the Scriptures not only contained the mystery of the suffering and
glorious Messiah, but they also prophesied the universal preaching of the
Church. "They become the basis for the testimony that the disciples are to
bear and the preaching that they are to carry out in his name."[13]

Consequently, Jesus entrusts to his disciples a mission that must reach
"all nations" (*panta ta ethnē*: Luke 24:47; cf. Matt 28:19 and Gen 22:18). What
did not occur during his earthly life will be realized in the time of the Risen
Christ—that is, in the time of the Church. The disciples will thus give definitive fulfillment to Israel's Scriptures and to God's saving plan. Nevertheless,
this mission must commence in Jerusalem; Luke, the evangelist of the pagan
world, insists on the importance of the holy city for the universal diffusion
of the gospel. What Isaiah proclaimed will thus be realized: "For out of Zion
shall go forth the law, and the word of the LORD from Jerusalem" (Isa 2:3).[14]
The universal proclamation of the gospel is inseparable from its reference
to Israel.

B. THE ACTS OF THE APOSTLES

The first scene of Acts presents a gathering of the Risen Christ with the
apostles in which they ask him: "Lord, will you at this time restore the kingdom to Israel?" (Acts 1:6). They continue to move in a particular rather than
universal perspective: Jesus is the liberator Messiah of Israel who restores
to Israel its ancient greatness. Jesus responds by diverting the attention to
the promised Spirit, which they will receive; the Spirit's effects on the disciples was to be decisive: "you shall be my witnesses in Jerusalem and in all
Judea and Samaria and to the end of the earth" (1:8b). These words of Jesus

---

13 Fitzmyer, *Luke*, 2:1580.

14 François Bovon, *Luke 3: A Commentary on the Gospel of Luke 19:28–24:53*, Hermeneia
(Minneapolis: Fortress, 2012), 396.

synthesize all of the subsequent narration, centered on the universal diffusion of the apostolic testimony.

"To the end of the earth" (*heōs eschatou tēs gēs*) is an expression from the book of Isaiah, where it appears in relation to the universal mission of the Servant of the Lord (Isa 49:6; cf. 48:20; 62:11). If we remember Simeon's prophecy, which alludes to this same biblical text in order to announce prophetically Jesus' mission, then we understand how the work commended by the resurrected Christ to his apostles is an extension and summit of his own mission, according to Luke.[15]

B.1. Pentecost (Acts 2)

The mission of the apostles is inaugurated on the day of Pentecost. The audience of Peter's first speech consists of Jews and proselytes (Acts 2:10–11), that is, of believers in the Jewish religion. They come from all parts of the empire (2:5).[16] Pentecost thus marks the beginning of a geographically universal mission. It is expressed in the gift of tongues, which foreshadows openness to the nations.[17] From her beginning, although localized in Jerusalem, the Church is shown to be a universal community.[18]

The speech of Peter that interprets the wonder that has occurred begins with the longest biblical citation in the whole book (Joel 3:1–5a; Acts 2:16–21). The pouring out of the Spirit "upon all flesh" is emphasized, with insistence on its universality: men and women, young and old, all the male and female servants of God will enjoy the effects of the Spirit (Acts 2:17–18). The prophet thus heralds the work of the Holy Spirit who, being the principal actor in

---

15 In his first speech, Paul will cite the prophecy of Isaiah 49:6, literally repeating the expression (Acts 13:47). "The expression *heōs eschatou tēs gēs* does not have a merely geographical meaning, but means universalism without limits." García Serrano, *The Presentation in the Temple*, 305.

16 "Many Jews of the diaspora, who were profoundly religious, went to Jerusalem to spend the last years of their lives, because they desired to be buried there." Jürgen Roloff, *Hechos de los Apóstoles*, BBC (Madrid: Cristiandad, 1984), 154. Fitzmyer, however, speaks of them as pilgrims who had come to Jerusalem to celebrate the feast: Joseph A. Fitzmyer, *The Acts of the Apostles: A New Translation and Commentary*, AB 31 (New York: Doubleday, 1998), 240.

17 "The gift of tongues enables the Twelve to proclaim the new Word of God to Israel, and eventually to all human beings." Fitzmyer, *Acts*, 237.

18 Charles K. Barrett, *The Acts of the Apostles*, 2 vols., ICC (Edinburgh: T&T Clark, 1994–98), 1:108.

Acts, will guide the young Church in her mission among the gentiles.[19] Finally, the prophetic citation concludes (Joel 3:5 [2:32 RSV]) by promising salvation for those who call upon "the name of the Lord" (Acts 2:21); this expression emphasizes the universal character of the gospel and thus anticipates the incorporation of the gentiles.[20] Let us note that "the Lord" now refers to Jesus (cf. Acts 2:36, 38): salvation is therefore decided according to faith in him. The question of submitting to the law of Moses, which will run throughout Acts as one of its fundamental themes, now receives a response that anticipates the eventual solution.[21] Baptism, and not the prescriptions of the law, is the principle of salvation; hence this salvation can be proposed to all human beings.[22] The episode of Pentecost thus becomes the foundation of the salvific universality to which Acts attests.

B.2. First Expansion of the Church (Acts 8)

The activity of the nascent Church is initially centered in Jerusalem but, little by little, she goes on to increase her radius of action. As a result of persecution, she will extend throughout Judea and Samaria (8:2), thus beginning to implement the *program* defined by Jesus in Acts 1:8. In Acts 8:4–25, Luke narrates the preaching in Samaria of the deacon Philip, who will be followed by Peter and John.[23] The openness to Samaria is already a beginning of universality; although the Samaritans had roots and traditions in common with Israel ("Our father Jacob": John 4:12), the Jews saw them as comparable to the pagans.[24] The function that this episode attributes to the Twelve is

---

19 "The Spirit . . . plays a significant role in deciding the nature and extent of the mission." O'Toole, *The Unity of Luke's Theology*, 29.

20 Marion L. Soards, *The Speeches in Acts: Their Content, Context, and Concerns* (Louisville, KY: John Knox, 1994), 33.

21 "A new criterion is established for belonging to the people of God; those who listen to Jesus, the prophet like Moses, belong to the people." O'Toole, *The Unity of Luke's Theology*, 29.

22 Baptism (following upon belief) is in effect the only condition for adhering to the Church: Acts 2:38; 8:12, 38; 9:18; 10:47–48; 16:15; 18:8; 19:5.

23 "The episode shows, then, how others than the Twelve become involved in bearing testimony to Christ." Fitzmyer, *Acts*, 400.

24 "Samaritans certainly were not regarded as true Jews." O'Toole, *The Unity of Luke's Theology*, 105. Cf. Matt 10:5: "Go nowhere among the Gentiles and enter no town of the Samaritans." The Samaritan healed of leprosy is called a "foreigner" by Jesus (*allogenēs*: Luke 17:18).

significant: their representatives, Peter and John, are the ones who complete the evangelization in Samaria. In the passage, the Samaritans' acceptance of the gospel is clear (8:8–14); at the end of the episode, the apostles themselves are the ones who evangelize many other small Samarian villages on their way back to Jerusalem (8:25). The episode of Simon the magician, on the other hand, implies the first encounter of the gospel with the religious mentality of the pagan world.[25] Simon is acclaimed as "that power [*dynamis*] of God which is called Great" (8:10); the narrator presents this *dynamis* in contrast with the Spirit, the true *dynamis* of God (Acts 1:8).[26] Simon accepts, although imperfectly, the superiority of the Spirit transmitted by Peter and John (8:18–24); his story anticipates that of the conversion of the pagans to the gospel, a conversion that—as we shall see in Ephesus (Acts 19)—will not be spared tensions and problems.

In this same chapter 8 of Acts, Philip is guided by an angel of God to the south, to the road that runs from Jerusalem to Gaza. There the conversion of a non-Jew, coming from a faraway land, is accomplished: an Ethiopian eunuch, a God-fearing man (cf. 8:27–28) who receives baptism at the hands of the deacon Philip (8:26–40).[27] In this way Luke reflects the universal reach of the Christian message, which little by little increases its radius of expansion.[28]

B.3. The Vocation of Paul (Acts 9; 22; 26)

In his encounter with Paul on the road to Damascus, the Risen Christ reveals to him his particular vocation, as we hear—in a different but concordant way—in each of the three reports of his conversion:

---

25 "In the Greek world of the time pagans could buy a role as priests in various religions; it was often sold to the highest bidder." Fitzmyer, *Acts*, 401. Later, in Cyprus, Saul and Barnabas will meet a similar person, a "Jewish false prophet" and "magician" named Bar Jesus or Elymas; Saul's (Paul's) censure of him will be decisive in the conversion of the proconsul Sergius Paulus (Acts 13:6–12).

26 The episode is in a certain way an anticipation of what will happen to Paul and Barnabas in Lystra, in a clearly pagan context (Acts 14:11–13). See also Acts 19 (in Ephesus).

27 Regarding whether this account is about a "God-fearing" pagan or a Jewish proselyte, cf. Roloff, *Hechos*, 192–93; Fitzmyer, *Acts*, 410.

28 Cf. O'Toole, *The Unity of Luke's Theology*, 105.

Go, for he is a chosen instrument of mine to carry my name before the Gentiles and kings and the sons of Israel. (Acts 9:15)

The God of our fathers appointed you to know his will, to see the Just One and to hear a voice from his mouth; for you will be a witness for him to all men of what you have seen and heard. (22:14–15)

But rise and stand upon your feet; for I have appeared to you for this purpose, to appoint you to serve and bear witness to the things in which you have seen me and to those in which I will appear to you, delivering you from the people and from the Gentiles—to whom I send you to open their eyes, that they may turn from darkness to light and from the power of Satan to God, that they may receive forgiveness of sins and a place among those who are sanctified by faith in me. (26:16–18)

In these reports Luke presents the vocation of Paul according to the prophetic model, especially that of Jeremiah and of the Servant of the Lord in Deutero-Isaiah.[29] Like them, Paul will be sent to Israel, but his announcement will consist in the fulfillment of the prophecies in Jesus and in their extension to the gentiles.

The apparition of the Risen Christ in the temple of Jerusalem confirms him in this mission: "Depart, for I will send you far away to the Gentiles" (22:21). The encounter with the Risen Christ makes him a witness (in fact in his letters he presents himself as an "apostle"); he is sent to the Jewish People *and* to the faraway nations, but with a particular dedication to the latter ("apostle to the Gentiles": Rom 11:13). The second part of Acts revolves around Paul's missionary journeys, as well as the last great journey—when he is a prisoner—to Rome. Through Saul, transformed into Paul (cf. Acts 13:9), the commandment of the Risen Christ will be realized: "you shall be my witnesses in Jerusalem and in all Judea and Samaria and to the end of the earth" (Acts 1:8).

B.4. A Decisive Moment:
the Baptism of Cornelius (Acts 10–11)

However, the question of the acceptance of the gentiles into the Church will be central in the narration of Acts, beginning with the episode of the

---

29 Wilson, *Gentile Mission*, 168. The allusion to diverse prophecies of the Old Testament is also a feature of Paul's accounts of his conversion in his letters.

centurion Cornelius, a pivotal event in the whole book (10:1–11:18).[30] The evangelization of the pagans, which is willed by God, is the central axis of the entire episode.[31] In a surprising vision (10:9–16), Peter is instructed about the necessity to go beyond the cultic prescriptions of the law in order to return to the order willed by the Creator, according to which every human being, by virtue of being human, can receive the gift of baptism without submitting to the law: "God has shown me that I should not call any man common or unclean" (10:28). A little later, Peter declares, "Truly I perceive that God shows no partiality, but in every nation anyone who fears him and does what is right is acceptable to him" (10:34–35). These words from the first among the Twelve, which are related to and amplify the universalism implicit in the speech at Pentecost, synthesize the teaching in the episode of Cornelius—and in the whole book—about this theme.[32] The Lord does not grant his grace by virtue of ethnic or ritual conditions, but by virtue of piety and works of justice. In order to obtain salvation, one is not required to submit to the law of Moses, but to have faith in Jesus Christ. The pouring out of the Holy Spirit upon these people, with signs similar to those of Pentecost, is considered by Peter to be a sign of the divine will, and it leads him to administer baptism to them (10:44–48). This decision leads to difficulties and serious reservations, as is shown by the repercussions that this episode has among the Jews of Jerusalem (11:1–3); overcoming the difficulties will not be easy.[33] But the action of the Spirit manifested in ecclesial life will greatly contribute to resolving these problems; the nascent and dynamic community

---

30 "The Cornelius episode is not just another conversion story, like that of the Ethiopian eunuch (8:26–40), for Cornelius and his household symbolize Gentiles, to whom testimony about the Christ-event now spreads, not just under the aegis of the leader of the Twelve, but at the direction of heaven itself." Fitzmyer, *Acts*, 447–48. "Luke has not omitted any element that could contribute to highlighting the significance of this event. Therefore, he has made this account the longest in the book." Roloff, *Hechos*, 223.

31 Czeslaw Lukasz, *Evangelizzazione e conflitto: Indagine sulla coerenza letteraria e tematica della pericope di Cornelio (Atti 10,1–11,18)*, EHS.T 484 (Frankfurt am Main: Peter Lang, 1993), 221.

32 Soards, *Speeches*, 73.

33 In fact, the entire episode of Cornelius is presented as a conflict between the divine will for universal salvation and the resistance from the circumcision party (Lukasz, *Evagelizzazione e conflitto*, 221).

of Antioch will be the first to integrate the gentiles into the Church as its common practice (Acts 11:19–26).

B.5. The Council of Jerusalem (Acts 15)

The question is again front and center in the narrative in Acts 15. Here the author states that despite everything that has transpired until then, some Christians coming from Judaism want to impose the law of Moses on the gentile converts in Antioch, disregarding what is already an accepted custom in the Antiochene church. Luke expresses it in a rudimentary way: "But some men came down from Judea and were teaching the brethren, 'Unless you are circumcised according to the custom of Moses, you cannot be saved'" (15:1). In the face of the scandal this causes, Paul and Barnabas go up to Jerusalem to confer with "the apostles and the elders," in what will eventually be known as the "Council of Jerusalem." There the Christians coming from Pharisaism again raise the question (15:5). A great debate ensues, but no human argument is able to settle the debate, save the charismatic intervention of Peter, whose argument is supported by his lived experience in the house of Cornelius. Peter affirms that justification comes through the grace of the Lord Jesus (15:7–11). Evoking his previous speeches, and explicitly recalling the conversion of Cornelius, he affirms that God makes no distinction between Jews and gentiles.[34] The testimony of Barnabas and Paul, which is also charismatic ("signs and wonders"), confirms that of Peter (15:12). Finally, James will corroborate this manifold testimony with that of Scripture; concretely, he cites part of the conclusion of the book of Amos, which speaks about the eschatological reconstruction of "the dwelling of David" with the salvation of the nations (Amos 9:11–12; Acts 15:13–21).[35] In this way he is able to reconcile the previously conflicting positions.[36] The final decision of the

---

34 Soards, *Speeches*, 91–92.

35 This perspective is visible above all in the Septuagint version, which is what Luke cites, and is distinct from the Hebrew text; see Roloff, *Hechos*, 309–10.

36 "Then it seemed good to the apostles and the elders, *with the whole Church* [*ekklēsia*], to choose men from among them" (Acts 15:22a; emphasis added). "James is the broadminded leader who, while basically agreeing with Peter about no circumcision and no obligation to observe the Mosaic law for Gentile Christians, seeks to preserve the unity and peace of the church." Fitzmyer, *Acts*, 553.

assembly of the apostles and elders is expressed in a letter that they confide to their envoys, Paul and Barnabas; significantly, the letter is addressed to the Christians coming from paganism (15:23). The assembly only requires that they "abstain from what has been sacrificed to idols and from blood and from what is strangled and from unchastity" (15:29).[37] The most probable interpretation is that these restrictions were set to avoid scandalizing the Jewish Christians (cf. 15:21).[38] James's intent is not to affirm the integral validity of the law of Moses for the newly baptized, but to facilitate coexistence between the Jewish Christians and the gentile Christians.[39] The four required precepts are based on Leviticus 17–18; the rabbinical tradition after the second century AD will include them among the so-called Noachide laws, that is, the moral duties the Bible prescribes for all human beings. The Jews are obligated to observe the Torah in its integrity while the rest of the human beings, who are "sons of the covenant of Noah" (cf. Gen 9), must respect certain fundamental requirements.[40]

The meeting in Jerusalem represents an important landmark in the Lukan narrative and hence in the extension of preaching of the gospel to the gentiles; the decision of the apostles and presbyters, in union with the Holy Spirit (15:28), will be confirmed by various interventions of heaven.[41] The two missionary journeys that Paul makes afterwards will be the concrete fulfillment of this decision. Now we will highlight some specific events.

37 The Greek word for "unchastity" is *porneia*, which is often interpreted as referring to illegitimate marriages. This meaning of the Hebrew *zěnût* is attested at Qumran. Fitzmyer, *Acts*, 557–58.

38 First Corinthians 8–10 amply addresses the theme of food sacrificed to idols, from a perspective that is not much different from the one we see here.

39 "James's regulations seek only a *modus vivendi* of Gentile among Jewish Christians and imply no salvific purpose in them." Fitzmyer, *Acts*, 557. Timothy's circumcision in Acts 16:3 has a similar motive.

40 "The seven Noachide laws as traditionally enumerated are: the prohibitions of idolatry, blasphemy, bloodshed, sexual sins, theft, and eating from a living animal, as well as the injunction to establish a legal system." *EncJud*, 15:284.

41 A little later Luke will speak about the vision of the Macedonian (gentile) who, in a dream, seeks Paul's help (16:9); he will interpret it as a divine sign (16:10).

B.6. Speech at the Areopagus (Acts 17)

After a fruitful but also turbulent journey through Philippi, Thessalonica, and Beroea (Acts 16–17) Paul arrives in Athens; there he stays alone, after sending a message to Silas and Timothy to come to him as soon as possible (17:15; cf. 1 Thess 3:1). Even though Paul also preaches in Athens to the Jews in the synagogue (17:17), the narrative centers on his contact with the gentile world. We have an antecedent in Paul's words addressed to the pagans in Lystra (Acts 14:15–17).[42] Now, however, in the cultural center of paganism, we see an organized presentation of the Christian faith for a gentile audience.

Luke recounts for us Paul's clash with pagan religiosity, which is very negatively described: a city "full of idols" (17:16), eager for novelties (17:21). Neither their religion nor their philosophies (Epicurean and Stoic) are open to the truth; Paul is, in their eyes, just another *babbler*, an announcer of exotic divinities ("Jesus and the resurrection": 17:18).[43] This initial presentation makes it possible to predict the overall, rather negative, result of Paul's preaching in Athens, which is of great importance. On the hill of the Areopagus, the ancient judicial supreme court in the classical period (next to the Acropolis), the apostle's testimony to the gentiles takes on a special solemnity.[44]

After a *captatio benevolentiae* (17:22), the speech takes as its point of departure Paul's walk through the streets of the city; that experience, described earlier by the narrator as something quite negative (17:16), is now centered on the most positive element: an altar with the inscription, "To the

42 "Most authors have given the speech at Lystra the literary function of preparing Paul's speech at Athens in chapter seventeen." Marianne Fournier, *The Episode at Lystra: A Rhetorical and Semiotic Analysis of Acts 14:7–20a*, AmUSt.TR 197 (New York: Peter Lang, 1997), 197–98. Cf. Soards, *Speeches*, 89–90.

43 The word *spermologos*, originally applied to birds that "pick up seeds," is a pejorative term for anyone who passes idly through public places looking for leftovers of goods that could be lying on the ground. From there, metaphorically speaking, it is applied to *charlatans*, which designates "one who learns lots of trivial things and wants to tell everyone about his knowledge." Johannes P. Louw and Eugene A. Nida, *Greek-English Lexicon of the New Testament, based on Semantic Domains* (Atlanta: Scholars Press, 1988), *sub voce*.

44 "It is the second most important Pauline speech in Acts." Fitzmyer, *Acts*, 601. The principal speech, addressed to the Jews of the diaspora, is given in the synagogue of Antioch of Pisidia (Acts 13). For a brief analysis of the speech in the Areopagus, see Luis Sánchez-Navarro, *Testimonios del Reino: Evangelios sinópticos y Hechos de los Apóstoles* (Madrid: Palabra, 2010), 251–55.

Unknown God" (17:23). It is paradoxical that the only salvageable part of the pagan religion would be the divinity that is unknown.[45] Paul sees in this altar to an "Unknown God" the possibility of preaching to them about the true God. The words that follow are a concrete ("canonical") example of dialogue between culture and the Christian faith.

The first part of the speech, which begins from this inscription, is without saying it explicitly, an exposition of the biblical doctrine about God the creator of the cosmos (17:24–25); we have already seen how biblical universalism is rooted in this doctrine. "The terminology that Paul employs is common to both Greek philosophical speculation and the OT";[46] the transcendence of the divinity, which is fundamental in biblical faith, is related to the philosophical vision.[47] Universal human fraternity is also characteristic of Greek philosophical thought, since the vision of reality as a cosmos that everything forms a part of involves understanding all of humanity as a universal family. Thus, this fraternity is founded on the community of origin of all human beings, as testified by the Bible (17:26).

Human existence as rooted in the divinity (17:28) is also an acceptable teaching for this type of philosophy. Paul goes on to bolster his argument by appealing to the authority recognized by his listeners, citing a work (*Phaenomena*) by the Greek poet Aratus of Soli, in Cilicia (310–240 BC).[48] "For we are indeed his offspring," that is, the offspring of God (17:28); "God is not only near to human beings, but they are related to him as kin."[49] The

---

45 Let us remember that in the Gospels, Jesus' evaluation of pagan religiosity was always negative.

46 Fitzmyer, *Acts*, 608. Pythagoras (582–507 BC) was the first to speak of the *kosmos*, or "ordered world"; Plato (427–347 BC) speaks of the creator and father of the universe; and Epictetus (AD 55–135) calls him "God." Philo of Alexandria will reformulate the Old Testament's teaching about God the creator with Greek philosophical terminology.

47 Plutarch (AD 50–120) tells us in his *Moralia* that Zeno of Citium (333–264 BC), the founder of Stoicism, taught that temples to the gods should not be constructed. A fragment of Euripides (480–406 BC) says, "What house fashioned by builders can contain the divine form within enclosing walls?" Fitzmyer, *Acts*, 608 n. 24.

48 The work *Phaenomena* is a Stoic poem inspired by Hesiod, which describes the constellations, the firmament, and other natural phenomena; it is composed of 1,154 hexameters. Cf. Aratus, *Phaenomena*, ed. Douglas Kidd, CCTC 34 (Cambridge: Cambridge University Press, 1997). In Titus 1:12 Paul cites the 6th-century Cretan poet Epimenides of Knossos.

49 Fitzmyer, *Acts*, 611.

Stoic idea that underlies this verse is of a pantheist nature, but its language is well adapted to the God of biblical revelation.[50] This allows Paul to reject idolatry and encourage conversion to the true God, who has manifested his magnanimity by tolerating these practices (17:29–30). Paul thus prepares the terrain for the final announcement, that of the resurrection of Christ, the universal judge (17:31). The frustrating result of the episode, which is manifested in the listeners' mocking and skeptical reaction (17:32), takes nothing away from its great value as evidence for a certain preaching of the gospel that is specifically addressed to pagans; in fact, some of them did believe (17:34). It is difficult to imagine a more expressive concretization of the universal call of the gospel of Jesus than this discourse of Paul; in fact, it provides the theological basis for the missionary push towards non-Jews.[51] What is required of them coincides substantially with what is required of the Jews: conversion and faith in Christ (cf. Acts 2:38).

B.7. Conflict in Ephesus (Acts 19)

Paul's stay in Ephesus, which lasted about three years and was very fruitful (Acts 19:18–20), in a way represents the culminating moment of his mission among the gentiles, but its conclusion will be disrupted by a conflict with the pagan cult of the protector goddess of the city, Artemis ("Diana" in the Roman pantheon; Acts 19:23–20:1).[52] The conflict originated with a revolt by the silversmiths who see their business endangered. The passage shows, however, that the problem cannot be reduced to economic concerns;

---

50 "The Zeus of these Stoic poets . . . is the *logos* or world principle which animates all things. . . . By presenting God as creator and judge, Paul emphasizes his personal character as opposed to the pantheistic Zeus of the Stoics." Frederick F. Bruce, *The Acts of the Apostles* (Grand Rapids, MI: Eerdmans, 1990), 385. "Paul understands the Stoic idea in a biblical sense; cf. Psalm 139; Luke 3:38 (Adam as God's son)." Fitzmyer, *Acts*, 611.

51 "God is no more circumscribed in the Jewish theological worldview. He is known and acknowledged by all." Chidi D. Isizoh, *The Resurrected Jesus preached in Athens: The Areopagus Speech* (Lagos: Ceedee Publications, 1997), 185.

52 Cf. Francis Pereira, *Ephesus: Climax of Universalism in Luke-Acts* (Anand, India: Gujarat Sahitya Prakash, 1983); Pereira highlights the fact that in Ephesus, for the first time, Paul will preach to the Jews and gentiles simultaneously (cf. Acts 19:10). "By the preaching of the gospel to both Jews and gentiles together on an equal footing, and with the consequent birth of the Christian community as a *tertium genus* in Ephesus, the Lucan Paul bridged the gulf between the two sections of mankind: the Jews and the gentiles." Pereira, *Ephesus*, 249–50.

on the contrary, the cult of the goddess is strongly rooted in the people (cf. 19:34).[53] The intervention of the city authorities will prevent the incident from escalating (19:31–40); in fact, these same authorities testify that Paul and his companions have not disobeyed the law of the city (19:37–40).[54] However, this episode highlights the real difficulties that the universal call of the gospel entails. There are many cultural and religious factors that resist and oppose it. In fact, in the affirmation of the silversmith Demetrius that "all Asia and the world worship" Artemis (19:27), one discovers a counterpoint to the gospel that Paul preaches; this account is about two cults with a claim to universality and that are incompatible with each other.[55] The fact that, in spite of everything, the word of the Lord grows and is powerfully strengthened (19:20) shows the lordship of the Spirit that invigorates that Word.

B.8. To the End of the Earth: Paul and Rome (Acts 25–28)

In Paul's time, Rome was synonymous with universality. As the capital of the empire, the whole empire was in a certain way present in it. For this reason, the goal of reaching Rome is an expression of the universal openness of the gospel. Already in Ephesus Paul expresses for the first time his desire to travel to Rome (19:21); this intention will be confirmed in Jerusalem by an apparition of the Lord: "Take courage, for as you have testified about me at Jerusalem, so you must bear witness also at Rome" (23:11). Paul will accomplish this word by using his status as a Roman citizen: facing the possibility of being judged by Festus in Jerusalem (25:9), with the consequent risk that the Jewish leaders will put pressure on him, he appeals to Caesar, before whom he should appear in court—in Rome, of course (25:11–12; cf. 28:19).[56] The last chapters of the book narrate the journey of Paul, a prisoner, to the

---

53 The ancient temple of Artemis in Ephesus (Artemision: 8th c.–356 BC) came to be one of the seven wonders of the ancient world; it was reconstructed as of 350 BC. Fitzmyer, *Acts*, 657.

54 This is another fact in the demonstration (which is significant in Acts) of the legitimacy of Christianity within the empire; cf. Fitzmyer, *Acts*, 655.

55 "Implied in such an assertion is the contrast with what Paul preaches, the message about the risen Christ, which is now making its way to 'the end of the earth' (1:8) and has even influenced many Ephesians." Fitzmyer, *Acts*, 656.

56 The *Lex Iulia de vi publica seu privata* protected Roman citizens throughout the empire from highhanded decisions of provincial governors; they thus had a right to be heard in Rome. Cf. Fitzmyer, *Acts*, 746.

imperial capital; there for a long time he will preach without impediment the kingdom of God—namely, he will teach "about the Lord Jesus Christ" (28:31). In this way the gospel achieves an unexpected diffusion; that announcement that at the beginning of the book was circumscribed by a small assembly in Jerusalem, a remote place in the empire, now resounds in the great metropolis. "Luke has reached the objective of his history by bringing Paul to Rome, where (albeit in custody) he enjoys complete liberty to preach the gospel. . . . The program mapped out in 1:8 has been carried through."[57]

C. CONCLUSION

The history narrated by Luke progresses from the particular to the universal, from salvation for Israel (Luke 1–2) to the universal diffusion of the gospel of Jesus (Acts). Let us note, however, something that we have already mentioned above. Universal openness does not lead us to consider Israel as henceforth irrelevant; on the contrary, Paul himself, at each stage of his journey (even in Rome, the final stage), preaches first to the Jews, and only afterwards to the pagans.[58] Once again the primacy of Israel in the announcement of the gospel is manifest; the historical Israel did not wish to receive this primacy, but it remains for Israel as a constant call to faith in the fullness of the covenant fulfilled in Jesus (cf. Rom 11:11–14). As Richard Bauckham puts it, "Luke's view of Israel and her future is open to (without requiring) a Pauline interpretation."[59] Frank Matera perceives this openness as a necessity: "As for the portion of Israel that continues to exist today without believing in Jesus as the Messiah, the Lukan view needs to be balanced by what Paul writes in Romans 9–11. God has not rejected his people (Rom 11:1), 'for the gifts and the calling of God are irrevocable' (11:29)."[60]

---

57 Bruce, *Acts*, 543. "How Paul's presence and activity in Rome encouraged gospel witness by other Christians in the city may be learned in his own words from Phil 1:12–18."

58 "The gospel was rightly and necessarily presented to the people of Israel first (*hymin prōton*, 3:26; 13:46)." Bruce, *Acts*, 63. Regarding this question see Jacques Dupont, *Teologia della Chiesa negli Atti degli Apostoli*, CSB 10 (Bologna: Dehoniane, 1984).

59 Richard Bauckham, "The Restoration of Israel in Luke-Acts" in *The Jewish World around the New Testament* (Grand Rapids, MI: Baker Academic, 2010), 370.

60 Frank J. Matera, *New Testament Theology: Exploring Diversity and Unity* (Louisville, KY: John Knox, 2007), 81.

CHAPTER FIVE

The Testimony of John

The fourth evangelist offers us a testimony of Jesus that is very unique; we now direct our attention to this Gospel. From its first page (the Prologue: John 1:1–18) the universal horizon of Jesus' work is made clear: "*all* things were made through him" (1:3); "The true light that enlightens *every man* was coming into the world" (1:9); "from his fulness we have *all* received, grace upon grace" (1:16). The salvation that Jesus brings is extended, therefore, to all humanity.

We should also note that while references to the chosen people are frequent, they are not without complexity. It is apparent that the Gospel of John has a notable Jewish tone; in contrast with the preceding Gospels, this Gospel mainly takes place in Jerusalem, a city about which John demonstrates a superior knowledge to that of the other evangelists.[1] The Jewish feasts demarcate the entire narration, thus giving it a particularly liturgical tonality.[2] Recent investigation is increasingly conscious of the genuinely Jewish background of the Gospel, which is undeniable.[3] At the same time,

---

1 Examples include Solomon's portico in the temple (cf. Acts 3:11; 5:12), the pool of Bethesda, the pool of Siloam, and the Kidron Valley.

2 Passover (John 2:13, 23; 6:4; 11:55); Tabernacles (7:2); Dedication (10:22); cf. Joseph Ratzinger (Benedict XVI), *Jesus of Nazareth: From the Baptism in the Jordan to the Transfiguration*, trans. Adrian J. Walker (New York: Doubleday, 2007), 236–38. The feast in John 5:1 is not specified, although it is probably Pentecost: Renzo Infante, *Le feste d'Israele nel Vangelo secondo Giovanni* (Cinisello Balsamo: San Paolo, 2010), 79–81. The presence of the Jewish feasts may reflect a characteristic of the Gospel author's personality: "The whole Johannine work is pervaded by an unmistakably cultic imprint precisely because, most likely, its author is a Levite priest." Infante, *Le feste*, 175.

3 Today, and especially after the discoveries of the Qumran, Bultmann's hypothesis (according to which the "ideological" background of John would be Gnosticism) has fallen into disuse.

however, we encounter in the Gospel a strong polemic against those whom the evangelist calls "the Jews," and we find expressions that lead us to think about a universal scope of the salvation wrought by Jesus. The faith manifested by the Samaritans ("the savior of the world": John 4:42) thus symbolically anticipates that openness: a direction in which the faith of the royal official, who was probably pagan, also points (4:50).

Regarding this second Cana sign, the hypothesis that the imperial official (Greek *basilikos*) of John 4:46–54 is a pagan, is plausible; Caesar is the only temporal king called *basileus* in the Fourth Gospel (John 19:15; cf. 19:12). Therefore, in John 3–4 we would have the sequence of Jew (Nicodemus)—Samaritan—pagan.[4] The synoptic parallel (the centurion: Matt 8:5–13 // Luke 7:1–10) points in this direction. On the other hand, many authors maintain that this official is at the service of Herod Antipas, tetrarch of Galilee, who in Matthew and Mark is inaccurately called *basileus* (Matt 14:9; Mark 6:14, 22, 25–27).[5] From this they conclude that the man must be Jewish.[6] But there would also have been pagans serving Herod, particularly among the soldiers;[7] it is possible, therefore, to postulate his status as a gentile. McHugh speaks of him as a gentile God-fearer: "If the *basilikos* in John is thus understood…, then this fourth and final section of John 3–4 completes the picture of the New Jerusalem by providing within it a prominent place for all who, though

---

The Gospel's strong Jewish roots are demonstrated in two directions: diachronic (Old Testament) and synchronic (contemporary Judaism). Cf. Domingo Muñoz León, "Evangelio según san Juan," in *Nuevo Testamento*, vol. 2 of *Comentario Bíblico Latinoamericano*, ed. Armando J. Levoratti (Estella, Spain: Verbo Divino, 2003), 597–98. For its targumic background, cf. Domingo Muñoz León, *Palabra y Gloria: Excursus en la Biblia y en la Literatura Intertestamentaria* (Madrid: CSIC-Instituto "Francisco Suárez," 1983), 17–33; John Ronning, *The Jewish Targums and John's Logos Theology* (Peabody, MA: Hendrickson, 2010).

4 Some authors think this way, for example, Secundino Castro Sánchez, *Evangelio de Juan: Comprensión exegético-existencial*, BTC 2 (Madrid: Universidad Pontificia Comillas, 2001), 129; Francis J. Moloney, *The Gospel of John* SP 4 (Collegeville, MN: The Liturgical Press, 1998), 160–61, although with reservations; Lorenzo Flori, *Le domande del Vangelo di Giovanni: Analisi narrativa delle questioni presenti in Gv 1–12* (Assisi: Cittadella, 2013), 239–40.

5 Raymond E. Brown, *The Gospel According to John I–XII*, AB 29 (Garden City, NY: Doubleday, 1966), 190.

6 Klaus Wengst, *Das Johannesevangelium: 1. Teilband: Kapitel 1–10*, TKNT 4/1 (Stuttgart: Kohlhammer, 2000), 177 n. 84; Hartwig Thyen, "Johannesevangelium," *TRE* 17 (1988): 203.

7 Cf. Rudolf Schnackenburg, *The Gospel According to St. John*, 3 vols., HTCNT (London: Burns & Oates, 1968–82), 1:465–66 and n. 16.

not of the Jewish race, shared in the worship of the people of Israel."[8] Next, we will uncover some passages that help us to go deeper into these questions.

A. "THE WORLD" IN JOHN

On the occasion of the conversation with Nicodemus in Jerusalem, the evangelist writes some especially dense words: "For God so loved the world that he gave his only-begotten Son, that whoever believes in him should not perish but have eternal life" (John 3:16). Even though the preceding context refers to an episode of Moses and the Israelites in the desert (John 3:14–15; cf. Num 21:8–9), the declaration just cited transcends a particular perspective and opens up a universal horizon. The motive of the Incarnation (cf. John 1:14), which is now presented as the Father's gift of the Son, is God's love for the world. And in the following verse the evangelist insists, "For God sent the Son into the world, not to condemn the world, but that the world might be saved through him" (3:17; cf. 1 John 4:9, 14). In this dense declaration, where John speaks about "eternal life" for the first time in the Gospel (vv. 15 and 16), he does not speak of the salvation of Israel but rather of the salvation of the world, understood as the whole of humanity—a humanity that is sinful and far from God.[9] What is required for accepting this salvation is not submission to the exigencies of the Torah, but faith in Jesus. The expression "whoever" (v. 16) highlights this universality.

"World" (*kosmos*) is an important concept in John; it appears 78 times (in Matt 9 times, Mark 3, Luke 3). From the beginning of the Gospel, the Baptist describes the mission of Jesus according to this broad horizon: "Behold, the Lamb of God, who takes away the sin *of the world*" (1:29).[10] In a similar way the Samaritans confess him to be "the savior of the *world*" (4:42). We

---

8 John F. McHugh, *John 1–4*, ICC (London: T&T Clark, 2009), 317.

9 "In general, the *kosmos* is not the totality of creation (11.9; 17.5, 24; 21.25 are exceptions) but the world of men and human affairs." Charles K. Barrett, *The Gospel According to St. John*, 2nd ed. (London: SPCK, 1978), 161. "The very first statement about God since the Prologue is that he *loved the world*, that is, the world seen 'existentially,' as it really is, full of sinfulness and estranged from its Maker." McHugh, *John*, 239.

10 In contrast, passages such as Matthew 1:21 and Luke 2:10–11 present Jesus' mission in relation to Israel. See also 1 John 2:2: "he is the expiation for our sins, and not for ours only but also for the sins of the whole world."

find a similar idea from the mouth of Jesus, in various forms: "the bread which I shall give for the life *of the world* is my flesh" (6:51); "I am the light *of the world*" (8:12); "I did not come to judge *the world*, but to save the world" (12:47). The salvation that Jesus brings is therefore meant for all human beings; already in the Prologue of the Gospel, John tells us that the Logos is "the true light that enlightens every man" (1:9). But then, what is the position of the Jewish People?

B. THE JEWS IN THE GOSPEL OF JOHN

The presentation of the Jews in the Fourth Gospel is not a simple question; the well-known expression of Charles K. Barrett, that "John is both Jewish and anti-Jewish,"[11] manifests the complexity of Jesus' relationship with his people and suggests that these categories ("Jewish" and "anti-Jewish") are insufficient to properly tackle the question.[12] For one thing, Jesus is identified with his people; this aspect becomes clear in his conversation with the Samaritan woman: "How is it that you, *a Jew*, ask a drink of me, a woman of Samaria?" (John 4:9; emphasis added); Jesus assumes this name naturally. From the context it is clear that "Jewish" refers not to a natural-born man of Judah but to a native of Galilee, so that one must understand it in a religious sense. The same can be applied to the *titulus crucis* ("king of the Jews": 19:19–21). Let us remember the commendation Jesus makes when introducing Nathanael: "Behold, an Israelite indeed, in whom is no guile!" (1:47). The authentic Israelite is one who turns away from sin and lives in the truth: "Blessed is the man to whom the lord imputes no iniquity, and in whose spirit there is no deceit" (Ps 32:2b); hence the only time that the term *Israēlitēs* appears in this Gospel it is comparable to a title of honor.[13]

---

11 Charles K. Barrett, *The Gospel of John and Judaism* (Philadelphia: Fortress, 1975), 71. A little earlier he affirms, "The fact is that this gospel contains Judaism, non-Judaism and anti-Judaism."

12 "Jew" in John is not a unidimensional person: Maurizio Marcheselli, "Il Vangelo di Giovanni nel giudaismo: Un'identità in tensione," *RivB* 61 (2013): 313.

13 "His verdict expresses a high esteem for Nathanael. The new arrival receives the honorable title of 'Israelite.'" Schnackenburg, *St. John*, 1:316.

In many passages, however, the expression "the Jews" has a clearly polemical connotation, designating those who do not believe in Jesus and refuse to accept him (cf. John 5:16, 18; 7:1; 8:48). On many occasions John speaks of the fear that they elicit.[14] "The Jews" acquire, so to speak, a paradigmatic and symbolic character: in the leaders' rejection of Jesus, the evangelist symbolizes all those who do not believe in him.[15]

Based on this fact, discussions about "anti-Judaism" or "anti-Semitism" in John have persisted and continue to this day.[16] In order to respond to this accusation we must consider various factors. First, a Gospel whose protagonist, Jesus, is openly designated as a Jew (4:9; cf. 4:22; 18:35) cannot be considered anti-Jewish.[17] Secondly, the polemic that runs through the Gospel is not a polemic of Christians versus Jews, but an internal polemic within Judaism; both the evangelist and Jesus are Jews.[18] Therefore, the paradigm for understanding this confrontation is the one that the prophetic books offer to us. Jesus confronts the leaders of his people *from the inside*; the difficult polemic that results is not more intense than the one that runs through certain passages of Isaiah, Jeremiah, or Ezekiel, for example.[19] In this respect, we appreciate that the polemical allusions to "the Jews" are always made in an intra-Jewish context; before those who do not belong to the people (the Samaritan woman or Pilate), Jesus is recognized—explicitly or implicitly—as a Jew. By acknowledging this fact, we can refute at its root any accusation that may conceive of this writing as hostile to Judaism. Jesus is a prophet

---

14 John 7:13; 9:22; 19:38; 20:19.

15 "Ceux que Jean appelle 'les Juifs' ne sont pas seulement les acteurs de ce drame: ils sont des 'types littéraires et théologiques' dans lequels chacun de nous peut se reconnaître" (Those whom John calls "the Jews" are not merely actors in this drama: they are "literary and theological types" in which each of us can recognize ourselves). Pierre Grelot, *Les Juifs dans l'Évangile de Jean*, CRB 34 (Paris: Gabalda, 1995), 182. Cf. Filippo Belli, "'I Giudei' nel vangelo secondo Giovanni. Come affrontare il problema," *RivB* 50 (2002): 63–75.

16 For a good synthesis, see Pontifical Biblical Commission, *The Jewish People*, §§ 76–78.

17 Marcheselli, "Il Vangelo di Giovanni nel giudaismo," 316–17. "Jésus se sent . . . inséré au cœur du Judaïsme: il est aussi juif que tout autre" (Jesus feels himself inserted in the heart of Judaism: he is as Jewish as any other). Grelot, *Les Juifs*, 172; see 171–75: "Jésus, le juif."

18 See Marcheselli, "Il Vangelo di Giovanni nel giudaismo," 299–302: "Il posto del QV è nel giudaismo?"

19 Regarding opposition to the leaders of Israel (a recurrent theme in the prophetic writings), see Isa 1:10–20; Jer 36; Ezek 34.

who, from within the people, seeks the conversion of those he debates with; John—also a Jew—aligns with this same approach.[20] This vision is confirmed by two Johannine passages, which we will study next.

C. THE JEWS AND SALVATION

After verifying Jesus' prophetic competence (4:19), the Samaritan woman raises the question of the religious division between the Jews and the Samaritans: "Our fathers worshiped on this mountain;[21] and you say that in Jerusalem is the place where men ought to worship" (4:20). Jesus responds with a sharp defense of Jewish worship in the face of Samaritan worship: "You worship what you do not know; we worship what we know…" (4:22b). When spoken by Jesus, this affirmation acquires undeniable significance: Jesus recognizes "the Jews" as beneficiaries of God's salvation. He says this, however, only after he helps the woman to understand also how his own ministry must transform that reality: "Woman, believe me, the hour is coming when neither on this mountain nor in Jerusalem will you worship the Father" (4:21). That "hour" is the "hour of Jesus" (see 13:1; 17:1). The recognition of the primacy of the Jewish People does not confer on it an absolute salvific value since the "hour" of Jesus will make a substantial change; at the same time, the new worship that will bring the old worship to its fulfillment is going to be realized through the action of Jesus—a member of that people. This is therefore about a singular member of the people, given that he is the divine Logos incarnate; "in this sense, also through the work of Jesus, 'salvation comes from the Jews,' since the God present in him is none other than the God of Israel."[22]

Hence, undoubtedly "salvation is from the Jews," but that salvation is not limited to them. As the Samaritans will affirm after welcoming Jesus for

---

20 Moreover, this does not exclude the possibility that the evangelist's frequent allusion to "the Jews" could potentially hint at the situation of the Christian community in his time. For this community, the Jewish People represents a reality that is clearly delineated and differentiated from the Church of the Messiah. See Marcheselli's exposition of this question, including interesting clarifications, in "Il Vangelo di Giovanni nel giudaismo," 318–20. It is noteworthy, however, that "Jew" never appears anywhere in John's letters.

21 Mount Gerizim, in Samaria.

22 Wengst, *Johannesevangelium*, 1:165.

two days, "we have heard for ourselves, and we know that this is indeed the Savior of the world" (4:42; cf. 1 John 4:14).

This reality is manifest in the evangelist's commentary on Caiaphas's words, in the prelude to the passion. The high priest affirms before the Sanhedrin: "You know nothing at all; you do not understand that it is expedient for you that one man should die for the people, and that the whole nation should not perish" (John 11:49b–50).[23] While these words appear starkly cruel in their obvious meaning,[24] the evangelist—in a paradigmatic case of Johannine "irony"[25]—explains them on another level of significance, in which they become prophetic: "He did not say this of his own accord, but being high priest that year he prophesied that Jesus should die for the nation, and not for the nation only, but to gather into one the children of God who are scattered abroad" (11:51–52).[26] These "children of God who are scattered abroad" are not, as one could perhaps think, only the Jews of the diaspora, but also the gentiles; they are the ones gathered together in the eschatological Israel, those whom Jesus previously mentioned as not belonging to the fold of Israel, but whom he must also shepherd.[27] "Jesus collects those who belong to him within and without Judaism, and lays down his life for them."[28] He will thus fulfill, in an unexpected way, the Old Testament prophecies that

23 The word for "people" (*laos*) is distinct from the word for "nation" (*ethnos*). Everything, however, seems to indicate that in John they function as synonyms, with no appreciable difference. Cf. Johannes Beutler, *Judaism and the Jews in the Gospel of John*, SubBi 30 (Rome: Pontifical Biblical Institute, 2006), 143.

24 Cf. John 11:53: "So from that day on they took counsel about how to put him to death."

25 Regarding the irony in John, see the explanation of Brown, *The Gospel According to John*, 1:cxxxvi: "The opponents of Jesus are given to making statements about him that are derogatory, sarcastic, incredulous, or, at least, inadequate in the sense they intend. However, by way of irony these statements are often true or more meaningful in a sense they do not realize." Cf. John 7:41–42.

26 "The high priest is involuntarily and unknown to himself uttering a prophecy." Rudolf Schnackenburg, *St. John*, 2:349.

27 Barrett, *Saint John*, 407. "Not all men but only those whom the Father has given to Jesus are God's children (8:42); and so the dispersed children of God are the Gentiles destined to believe in Jesus." Brown, *The Gospel According to John*, 1:440; cf. 443. "And I have other sheep, that are not of this fold; I must bring them also, and they will heed my voice" (John 10:16). "The Gentile mission is itself an activity of Christ, just as his ministry in Palestine was." Barrett, *Saint John*, 376.

28 Barrett, *Saint John*, 407–8.

depict the gentiles flocking to Mount Zion: "When through Jesus' death his body becomes the new temple, naturally he serves as the focus for gathering together the Gentiles."[29]

> The evangelist [in 11:52] is deliberately broadening the Jewish perspective, but even then he does not simply say "for the world" (cf. 1 John 2:2), but chooses words which allow his idea of the true Israel (cf. 12:13 with 12:19) to show through. It is as though he transcends the word *ethnos* with its restriction to the Jewish people of the time, and puts in its place the idea of the eschatological Israel, which will once more include the twelve tribes and will be gathered out of the dispersion. This prophecy of salvation, so important in the prophetic books of the Old Testament, lies unmistakably behind the evangelist's words. In his attitude to the pagan world, however, he does not retain the original idea of the pagans streaming to God's holy mountain Zion, the incorporation of the nations into the people of the God of Israel, but adopts the further developed ecclesiological view that a single new people of God made up of Jews and Gentiles is already being formed as a result of Jesus' death. It is not the tribes of Israel who are to be gathered out of the dispersion, but the "children of God."[30]

The two passages, the dialogue with the Samaritan woman and the words of Caiaphas, offer an image suitable for the Johannine understanding of the Jewish people. Beyond the polemics with the people represented by their leaders, Jesus affirms that "salvation comes from the Jews." This is predicated on a recognition of the election of Israel and the revelation that it has received, but it also implies an anticipation of Israel's proper mission, which the evangelist will discover to be manifested in the words of the high priest. Because Jesus is Jewish, and because he is a lofty member of this people, "salvation comes from the Jews"; to them the salvation that he brings is directed first ("that Jesus should die for the nation": 11:51), but that salvation is not only for the chosen people but it also extends to all human beings: to the "sheep that are not of this fold" (10:16), to the "children of God who are scattered abroad" (11:52), to those who, by means of the word of the disciples, will believe in Jesus (17:20).

---

29 Brown, *The Gospel According to John*, 1:443.
30 Schnackenburg, *St. John*, 2:350.

D. SALVATION FOR THE GENTILES

A little after the words of Caiaphas, an episode that is relevant for our purposes takes place: for the first time some gentiles, explicitly presented as such, come and request to see Jesus (John 12:20–22).[31] The evangelist specifies that they are "some Greeks"; they are thus non-Jews. Be they proselytes or "God-fearers," they represent the pagan world.[32] Jesus' response is enigmatic; after affirming that the hour of being glorified has arrived, by which we can infer a positive reaction to the Greeks' request (12:23), he announces his future death through the allegory of the grain of wheat (12:24), a death that is presented as a guarantee of fruitfulness. He seems to not respond to the desire of those who seek him; on the contrary, he is indicating the mode in which it will be possible for the Greeks to see him just as he should be seen, that is, with faith. Therefore he interprets the arrival of these men as a sign that the moment for him to give his life has arrived.[33] He affirms this a little later in the same scene: "and I, when I am lifted up from the earth, will draw all men to myself" (12:32); we thus understand that *much* fruit (12:24) refers to *all*: to the multitude of the saved, which is why it anticipates universal salvation. The episode therefore has great importance in the Gospel.[34] The "hour" of Jesus, a theme that dominates the stories of the passion in Saint John, is the moment of the universal openness of his saving work.[35]

Being "lifted up" is the way in which Jesus refers to his future death (cf. John 3:14; 8:28; 12:32). This closely connects the universal openness of the gospel with the paschal mystery of Jesus. The Greeks will "see" him, but to this end they should wait until he is "lifted up from the earth." In that moment

---

31 In the Gospel narrative they are preceded by the "royal official" of John 4:46–54; see what is said above.

32 "The horizon is widened to all those who lived in the Greek world." Muñoz León, "San Juan," 650. Cf. Hye J. Lee, *"Signore, vogliamo vedere Gesù": La conclusione dell'attività pubblica di Gesù secondo Gv 12,20–36*, TGST 124 (Rome: Editrice PUG, 2005), 170–71, 193. Along the same lines are Moloney, *The Gospel of John*, 351–52; Klemens Stock, *Gesù il Figlio di Dio: Il messaggio di Giovanni*, BibPr 16 (Rome: Edizioni ADP, 1993), 121; Castro Sánchez, *Evangelio de Juan*, 279.

33 "We are told that the hour has come. Evidently the coming of the Greeks has indicated this." Brown, *The Gospel According to John*, 1:470.

34 "The *coming* of the Gentiles is so theologically important that the writer never tells us if they got to see Jesus, and indeed they disappear from the scene in much the same manner that Nicodemus slipped out of sight in ch. 3." Brown, *The Gospel According to John*, 1:470.

35 Cf. John 12:27; 13:1; 17:1; 19:27.

of the Passion the evangelist will discover the fulfillment of Scripture: "They shall look on him whom they have pierced" (19:37; cf. Zech 12:10). In this way the addressees of John's Gospel, those to whom he directs this writing "so that you may believe" (John 20:31), are all Christians without distinction: both those coming from Judaism and those from gentile background, all those who have been "born from on high" (cf. 3:3) by means of baptism. The paschal mystery, the "hour" of Jesus, has banished all differences with regard to salvation.[36]

E. CONCLUSION

Our study of selected Johannine passages shows us how John understands the universal scope of Jesus' mission. It is something that pervades the entire Gospel account, beginning with the Prologue, and that is manifested in its most intense moments. Jesus is the light of the world (8:12); he himself speaks of his passion in unequivocally universal terms: "and I, when I am lifted up from the earth, will draw all men to myself" (12:32). What is latent in the other Gospels and comes to the surface only in certain moments, is constantly present in the Fourth Gospel. The salvation that Jesus brings does not exclude anyone: all human beings, from all times (cf. 17:20), are called to believe in him.

But this universal salvation, which assumes the transformation of Israel, does not imply that the chosen people disappears or is reduced to irrelevance. As with the other New Testament writings, we can verify in John how the universal openness of Jesus' gospel does not entail a devaluation of Israel, but rather a maximum appreciation of it. Only this Gospel, which through the Samaritan woman calls Jesus a "Jew," has transmitted to us a declaration by this same Jesus that is as transcendental as the one already mentioned: "salvation is from the Jews." Despite the substantial change that the "hour" of Jesus will bring for the people of the covenant, a greater mission than that of Israel cannot be conceived: to be a mediator for all humankind to reach this salvation.

---

36 "John was not interested in Gentiles as distinct from Jews, or in Jews as distinct from Gentiles or Samaritans, because all ethnic categories had lost significance." Raymond E. Brown, *An Introduction to the Gospel of John*, ed. Francis J. Moloney, ABRL (New York: Doubleday, 2003), 181.

CHAPTER SIX

The Testimony of Paul

To speak of the universal dimension of the salvation brought by Christ, and consequently the universality of the Church, is to speak of Paul. No one has concretely incarnated and fulfilled this dimension of the Christian community as he has. Therefore, an adequate treatment of this question would require a reading of all his letters. Our exposition, however, will focus on four fundamental points: a) Paul, a Jewish apostle to the gentiles; b) the universality of sin and of salvation in Christ; c) Jews and gentiles in Paul; and d) the situation of Israel.

A. PAUL, A JEWISH APOSTLE TO THE GENTILES

Despite coming from a gentile land (Tarsus of Cilicia), Paul is Jewish by birth, as he firmly states: "circumcised on the eighth day, of the people of Israel, of the tribe of Benjamin, a Hebrew born of Hebrews; as to the law a Pharisee, as to zeal a persecutor of the Church, as to righteousness under the law blameless" (Phil 3:5–6).[1] All the testimonies highlight the militant Judaism of the young Saul.[2] We thus find ourselves faced with a genuine representative of the people of the covenant in the first age of the New Testament. His encounter with the Risen Jesus on the road to Damascus, however,

---

1 Cf. Rom 11:1b: "I myself am an Israelite, a descendant of Abraham, a member of the tribe of Benjamin"; "Are they Hebrews? So am I. Are they Israelites? So am I. Are they descendants of Abraham? So am I" (2 Cor 11:22). See also Acts 22:3; 23:6; 26:5.

2 "For you have heard of my former life in Judaism, how I persecuted the Church of God violently and tried to destroy it; and I advanced in Judaism beyond many of my own age among my people, so extremely zealous was I for the traditions of my fathers" (Gal 1:13–14). Cf. Acts 9:1; 22:4–5, 19–20; 26:9–11.

leads to a radical change in his life, which will cause him to reconsider his whole life in the new light of Christ. Therefore—without abandoning his Jewish practice—he can affirm that "I count everything as loss because of the surpassing worth of knowing Christ Jesus my Lord" (Phil 3:8), to the point that he is considered particularly destined to preach the gospel among the pagans, coming to be called "apostle to the Gentiles" (*ethnōn apostolos*: Rom 11:13).[3] All of his letters are addressed to communities outside of Palestine, whose majority is formed by Christians coming from a gentile background.[4]

The revelation received by Paul has allowed him, therefore, to take the step that Israel's Scriptures had prophesied. As we recall, these Scriptures spoke of a salvation that, mediated by the chosen people, would reach all nations. The Twelve and the Church gathered around them fulfill this promise, but Saul, the fervent Jew of the tribe of Benjamin (like Saul, the first king of Israel), will be a member of the chosen people who is particularly called to incarnate this fulfillment. By doing this he does not betray his roots, but he achieves his proper fullness as a son of Israel; it was necessary that the "apostle to the Gentiles" should be an authentic son of Israel, in order thus to manifest its eschatological openness, just as—according to Acts—he will proclaim to the Jewish community of Rome: "it is because of the hope of Israel that I am bound with this chain" (Acts 28:20). In his particular vocation of service to the gentiles, Paul does not find a negation of his Jewish condition but a full realization of it.

B. UNIVERSALITY OF SIN AND OF SALVATION IN CHRIST (ROM 5)

The first three chapters of the Letter to the Romans place before our eyes the situation of humanity before Christ: not only the gentiles (Rom 1), but also the Jews—despite the gift of the Law (Rom 2)—have allowed themselves

---

3 William S. Campbell, " 'I Rate All Things as Loss': Paul's Puzzling Accounting System: Judaism as Loss or the Re-evaluation of All Things in Christ?," in *Celebrating Paul: Festschrift in Honor of Jerome Murphy-O'Connor, O.P., and Joseph A. Fitzmyer, S.J.*, ed. Peter Spitaler, CBQMS 48 (Washington, DC: The Catholic Biblical Association of America, 2011), 39–61. Cf. Rom 1:5; 11:13; Gal 1:16; 2:8; Eph 3:8; 1 Tim 2:7. See especially Rom 15:15–16.

4 Cf. Rom 1:13; Eph 2:11; 3:1; Col 1:27.

to be carried away by the sin that leaves them in a negative situation before God.[5] Therefore, concludes Paul, "all have sinned and fall short of the glory of God" (Rom 3:23). He expounds on this perspective in chapter 5, which elaborates on the effects of the first sin for all humanity: "Therefore as sin came into the world through one man and death through sin, and so death spread to all men because all men sinned" (Rom 5:12). A man, Adam (cf. v. 14), introduced sin, and as a consequence all human beings, in solidarity with Adam, sinned in turn.[6] This is properly perceived in light of the work of Christ, just as a fundamental verse reveals: "For as by one man's disobedience many were made sinners, so by one man's obedience many will be made righteous" (5:19).[7] The universal salvation enacted by Christ makes manifest that disastrous influence that sin had on our first parents, and that by virtue of the solidarity that exists among all human beings affects all of humanity.[8] The justification received, on the contrary, has put human beings at peace with God (5:1) and is therefore cause for hope in the definitive universal justification: "many will be made righteous" (Rom 5:19).[9] This solid theological foundation allows us to focus now on the distinct roles of Jews and gentiles in the order of salvation, according to the apostle to the gentiles.

C. JEWS AND GENTILES IN PAUL

Let us note first of all that, just as Acts describes to us and as can be concluded also from his letters, Paul's preaching is addressed first to the Jews; in all stages of his evangelization, he preaches first to the children of Israel, and only afterwards to the gentiles. Therefore, the title "apostle to the Gentiles" designates the most characteristic dimension of the apostle, but it

---

5 For insight on this theme in the Pauline letters, see Frank J. Matera, *God's Saving Grace: A Pauline Theology* (Grand Rapids, MI: Eerdmans, 2012), 88–102: "Humanity apart from Christ."

6 Cf. Frank J. Matera, *Romans*, Paideia (Grand Rapids, MI: Baker Academic, 2010), 137.

7 "In light of Christ's obedience, which has made the many righteous, Paul concludes that Adam's transgression made the many sinners." Matera, *Romans*, 140.

8 Cf. Alfonso Lozano Lozano, *Romanos 5: La vida de los justificados por la fe y su fundamento, la reconciliación por nuestro Señor Jesucristo*, ABE 56 (Estella, Spain: Verbo Divino 2012), 161–227: "Rom 5,12: La obra de Adán y sus consecuencias universales."

9 Cf. Lozano Lozano, *Romanos 5*, 273–75.

is not exclusive. As Paul himself says, "I have become all things to all men, that I might by all means save some" (1 Cor 9:22; cf. vv. 20–21).

C.1. The Primacy of the Jews

Being an apostle to the gentiles does not mean that for Paul being a Jew or gentile is a matter of indifference. In his letters, Paul testifies to the notable difference between one and the other; for him, "Jew" and "gentile" are not abstract concepts, but they respond to the daily reality that surrounds him and also defines the existence of the Christian communities, formed by persons coming from one or the other origin. Paul does not hesitate to affirm that the Jews are the chosen people, while the gentiles are deprived of the saving knowledge of God: "We ourselves, who are Jews by birth and not Gentile sinners..." (Gal 2:15). In the letter to the Romans, Paul delights in recalling the privileges the chosen people enjoy: "They are Israelites, and to them belong the sonship, the glory, the covenants, the giving of the law, the worship, and the promises; to them belong the patriarchs, and of their race, according to the flesh, is the Christ, who is God over all, blessed for ever. Amen" (Rom 9:4–5).[10]

To negate the prerogatives of Israel, which make it a unique reality in the history of humanity, would be to close oneself off from the evidence; Paul is conscious that the gifts received by the chosen people, of whom he is honored to be a part, constitute an immense richness that differentiates it from the other nations on earth.[11] He also understands that the Jewish people already possessed, in hope, Christ himself: the Jews are those "who first hoped in Christ" (Eph 1:12).[12] Apart from that, the fact of having made

10 Cf. Rom 2:17–20. Later we will delve into Romans 9–11, which treats the situation in which the Jews have remained after the coming of Christ.

11 He reminds the Ephesians, for example, of their sad state before their conversion: "alienated from the commonwealth of Israel, and strangers to the covenants of promise" (Eph 2:12).

12 "They already had Christ, in a certain sense, in the Torah and in the prophets and in the promise of God, Rom 3:21; Gal 3:16. They had him also hidden, in a quasi-sacramental form, during the wandering in the desert, in the rock that followed them, 1 Cor 10:4." Heinrich Schlier, *Carta a los Efesios: Comentario*, BEB 71 (Salamanca: Sígueme 1991), 157. In contrast to them, the pagans were "without Christ" (Eph 2:12).

possible the coming of the Messiah (cf. Rom 9:5) confers on Israel a unique significance for the history of humanity.[13]

The salvific primacy of Israel does not, however, exclude universal salvation, but rather is the foundation of it. This is shown clearly in another passage of the letter to the Romans:

> For I tell you that Christ became a servant to the circumcised to show God's truthfulness, in order to confirm the promises given to the patriarchs, and in order that the Gentiles might glorify God for his mercy. As it is written, *Therefore I will praise you among the Gentiles, and sing to your name* [Ps 18:50]; and again it is said, *Rejoice, O Gentiles, with his people* [Deut 32:43]; and again, *Praise the Lord, all Gentiles, and let all the peoples praise him* [Ps 117:1]; and further Isaiah says, *The root of Jesse shall come, he who rises to rule the Gentiles, in him shall the Gentiles hope* [Isa 11:10]. (Rom 15:8–12)

On the one hand, Christ directed his ministry to the Jews, says Paul (let us recall Matt 10:5 and 15:24), in order to show God's fidelity to his covenant and to bring the promises to fulfillment. On the other hand, the incorporation of the gentiles into the people of God is the work of God's boundless mercy, a mercy testified by the Torah, the Prophets, and the Writings: the various testimonies show the importance of this doctrine. But God, in his mercy, does not dispense that salvation to them apart from the chosen people; on the contrary, "the pagans obtain justification and salvation insofar as they participate in the privileges of Israel."[14] Let us see how.

C.2. The Gentiles and Salvation

The extent of this divine mercy can be appreciated from the historical situation of the pagans. In the letter to the Ephesians Paul says, "And you he made alive, when you were dead through the trespasses and sins in which you once walked, following the course of this world" (Eph 2:1–2). Before Christ,

---

13 Tatum also maintains that in the letter to the Romans, Paul defends the privileges of the Jewish People as opposed to the Christians coming from paganism, who might underestimate the dietary and festival practices of the Jews and Jewish Christians of Rome. Gregory Tatum, "'To the Jew First' (Romans 1:16): Paul's Defense of Jewish Privilege in Romans," in Spitaler, *Celebrating Paul*, 275–86.

14 Stanislas Lyonnet, *La historia de la salvación en la carta a los romanos* (Salamanca: Sígueme, 1967), 16.

the Ephesians were dead in terms of their relationship with God.[15] Regarding what he then says to this community of Christians coming in large part from paganism, it is concluded that the gentiles are human beings without hope who live far from God: "having no hope and without God [*atheoi*] in the world" (Eph 2:12).[16] The Ephesians had not been "atheists" in the strict sense, as Paul tells them: they had gods.[17] Their entry into Christ, however, has made them see their previous situation in a new way. The religious world at that time, particularly in Asia Minor, was a colorful "bazaar" in which the most diverse deities intermixed.[18] On more than a few occasions this resulted in a syncretism that gave the appearance of religiosity but left people in the most absolute perplexity before the mystery of the divine—an impassable abyss, in the face of the lack of communication from the *beyond*. How can one have something like hope if the fundamental mysteries of existence remain totally opaque? We can thus understand the radicality of Paul's words: in reality, those who believe in many gods (*theoi*) are "atheists" (*atheoi*), since they are closed off from the true God and they are lost in the multitude of divinities that compose the Greco-Roman pantheon.[19] This results in a religiosity that is repugnant to reason. In the first letter to the Corinthians, Paul reminds them of their previous situation, which is certainly lamentable: "You know that when you were heathen, you were led astray to mute idols" (1 Cor 12:2).

Writing to the Romans from Corinth, Paul will offer a deeper analysis of the dramatic irrationality of idolatry: "they became fools and exchanged the glory of the immortal God for images resembling mortal man or birds or

15 Matera, *God's Saving Grace*, 95.

16 Cf. 1 Thess 4:13: "But we would not have you ignorant, brethren, concerning those who are asleep, that you may not grieve as others do who have no hope." "In [Eph] 2:12 Paul lists five theological disadvantages of the Gentiles, and all except the last, summative item ('without God in the world') are related to the Gentiles' lack of access to the Scriptures." Frank Thielman, *Ephesians*, BECNT (Grand Rapids, MI: Baker Academic, 2010), 151.

17 "The very term Paul uses here, ἄθεος (*atheos*, without God), was used with disdain by Gentiles to describe the Jews, who refused to worship their gods." Thielman, *Ephesians*, 157.

18 Let us recall the tribulations Paul suffered in Ephesus because of the cult of Artemis (Acts 19:23–41).

19 "From their own perspective, many Gentiles would have claimed to be piously devoted to the gods." Thielman, *Ephesians*, 157; however, "the numerous gods of the pagans and the worship paid to them are precisely the proof that the pagans lived 'without God.'" Schlier, *Efesios*, 159.

animals or reptiles" (Rom 1:23). He sketches the dismal landscape generated by this perversion of religiosity: the generalized diffusion of sexual disorder and the rest of the vices (Rom 1:24–32). The pagans, in effect, are "sinners" (let us recall Galatians 2:15, cited above). But despite everything, Paul will forcefully proclaim that salvation, mediated in history by the chosen people, is also for the non-Jews. What is the basis for this?

C.3. A New Understanding of Scripture

At the conclusion of the letter to the Romans we read the following:

> Now to him who is able to strengthen you according to my gospel and the preaching of Jesus Christ, according to the revelation of the mystery which was kept secret for long ages but is now disclosed and through the prophetic writings is made known to all nations, according to the command of the eternal God, to bring about the obedience of faith—to the only wise God be glory for evermore through Jesus Christ! Amen. (Rom 16:25–27)

The Pauline vision of history is condensed into these lines.[20] The salvation of the gentiles belongs to the eternal disposition of the eternal God, but until the appearance of Jesus it had remained in "mystery": Paul employs this term in order to refer to that divine plan contained in the Old Testament but clearly formulated only by the preaching of the gospel. That *mysterion*, which consists in the salvation of all nations through "obedience of faith," has been made known "through the prophetic writings"; it is Scripture itself, read in light of Jesus' resurrection, that has made that plan clear—a plan that is present yet hidden, "silent," in Sacred Scripture. Already at the beginning of this letter, Paul had referred to the gospel as something "promised beforehand through his prophets in the holy Scriptures" (Rom 1:2). The testimony of Scripture ends up being fundamental for understanding the necessary openness of the gospel to the nations.

As Paul says elsewhere, however, Christians are the ones who are capable of reading the true meaning of Scripture, which is veiled for those who do not believe in Jesus:

---

20 Regarding the textual problem posed by the placement of these verses within the letter, cf. Bruce M. Metzger, *A Textual Commentary on the Greek New Testament*, 2nd ed. (Stuttgart: Deutsche Bibelgesellschaft, 1994), 470–73, 476–77.

But their minds [referring to the children of Israel] were hardened; for to this day, when they read the old covenant, that same veil remains unlifted, because only through Christ is it taken away. Yes, to this day whenever Moses is read a veil lies over their minds; *but when he turns to the Lord the veil is removed* [cf. Exod 34:34]. Now "the Lord" is the Spirit, and where the Spirit of the Lord is, there is freedom. (2 Cor 3:14–17)

Read outside of the resurrection of Christ, Scripture remains veiled, so that it becomes impossible to read its plan of universal salvation. The Risen Christ destroys the veil; Paul, who has experienced this, has been made capable of understanding that plan, and from now on he will dedicate all his strength to fulfilling it. Scripture is thus revealed by Paul as a true prophecy of Christ; its cultic and institutional dimensions are shown as passing elements whose force proceeds from that prophetic character that in Christ has reached its *telos* (cf. Rom 10:4).[21]

But in order for the divine plan to come to light—or better, in order for it to be fulfilled—Christ's redemptive act is necessary. Paul describes this in the letter to the Ephesians, where he pays special attention to its consequences for the gentiles.

C.4. The Work of Christ: To Break Down the Wall (Eph 2)

Before Jesus, an insuperable distance separated the Jews and the gentiles; the former were close to God, while the latter were far from him.

According to Paul, humanity falls into two groups, no matter how unequal they may be in number and size: Jews and Gentiles. That is not a sort of short-sighted nationalism on the part of Paul the Jew. It is the way that God sees mankind, God, in whose eyes number and mass have no value. On account of its election and the mystery of its mission, the chosen people of God, in spite of its smallness, outweighs by far the heathen world, no matter how innumerable its peoples.[22]

---

21 "According to Paul and to Hebrews, the Old Testament as prophecy announces its own end as an institution; the Old Testament as revelation manifests the provisional nature of its legislation." Albert Vanhoye, "Salut universel par le Christ et validité de l'Ancienne Alliance," *NRTh* 116 (1994): 819.

22 Max Zerwick, *The Epistle to the Ephesians*, trans. Kevin Smyth (New York: Herder and Herder, 1969), 46. The expression varies: "Jews and Greeks" (Rom 1:16; 2:9–10; 3:9; 1 Cor 10:12; 12:13; Gal 3:28; Col 3:11) or "Jews and Gentiles [*ethnē*]" (Rom 3:29; 9:24; Gal 2:14–15). Both

Therefore, in principle the pagans could not benefit from the divine promises. The passion of Christ, however, has made possible what was impossible before: "But now in Christ Jesus you who once were far off have been brought near in the blood of Christ" (Eph 2:13).

The blood of Christ, which has sealed the new covenant (cf. 1 Cor 11:25) and has brought about universal peace (cf. Col 1:20), has made it possible for the pagans to be close to God.[23] The adverbs *makran* (far off) and *engys* (near) are here indebted to Isa 57:19, which will be alluded to in Eph 2:17. In its original context, the Isaianic passage refers to Jews wherever they might be, but the wider context in Isaiah frequently emphasizes the unification of Israel with all peoples in the worship of God (Isa 55:5; 56:6–8); thus, Paul could have understood it as a prophecy of the inclusion of gentiles within God's people through the gospel.[24] Already in the letter to the Romans, Paul explained that the blood of Christ is the source of justification: that justification (by faith and not by works) which equally affects Jews and gentiles (Rom 5:9). "God bestowed his closeness on the ancient pagans by means of Christ's expiatory blood, shed on the cross."[25]

Next, Paul explains, now in the first person (therefore including himself among the beneficiaries of Christ's action), what being "brought near" means:

> For he is our peace, who has made us both [Jews and gentiles] one, and has broken down the dividing wall of hostility, by abolishing in his flesh the law of commandments and ordinances, that he might create in himself one new man in place of the two, so making peace, and might reconcile us both to God in one body through the cross, thereby bringing the hostility to an end. And he came and preached peace to you who were far off and

---

pairings are equivalent, as 1 Cor 1:22–24 shows ("Jews and Greeks" in vv. 22 and 24; "Jews and Gentiles" in v. 23). In 1 Cor 10:32, "Jews" and "Greeks" are distinguished from "the Church of God." Although Ephesians belongs to the Pauline corpus, its authorship is disputed (see John Gillman, "The Letter to the Ephesians," in *JBC XXI*, 1664); however, "since there are no compelling reasons to the contrary, this interpreter [Gillman] advocates the traditional position of Pauline authorship" (ibid). Ephesians "makes sense as an authentic letter from Paul to Christians in Ephesus, written at the end of a lengthy period of imprisonment and thus after nearly all of his undisputed correspondence." Thielman, *Ephesians*, 5.

23 "Christ signals the 'place' where one is close to God. Christ himself is the 'space' in which one is given this closeness to God." Schlier, *Efesios*, 160.

24 Thielman, *Ephesians*, 158.

25 Schlier, *Efesios*, 160.

peace to those who were near; for through him we both have access in one Spirit to the Father. (Eph 2:14–18)

What before was enmity—a wall that radically separated—is now peace and communion between the two and with God. "Raising them from a religious nothingness, *passing by* all the religious riches of Israel, God takes the heathen to his heart, on the same footing as the children of his election! This for many a Jewish heart was simply unbelievable. It was the gravest scandal. But for Paul it was *the* mystery of God, which he is now never tired of praising."[26] Through his cross, Christ has made possible the integration of Jews and gentiles in a single divine plan (v. 16).[27] This peace is the "gospel" that Jesus brought (v. 17), and it represents a radical new thing—a new creation (v. 15; cf. 2:10, "created in Christ Jesus"). Moreover, this peace and this gospel are Jesus himself, who thus fulfills the expectations of the book of Isaiah (cf. Isa 9:5; 52:7); all the good things of salvation are concentrated in him.[28]

Christ has accomplished this in "abolishing in his flesh the law of commandments and ordinances" (v. 15). This statement is about the law that consists of commandments and is expressed in them.[29] It is not, therefore, the law understood as revelation, but the law seen as a collection of norms that concretely characterize the life of the Jewish people.[30] Thus understood, the law is something negative in Paul.

> The characterization of the commandments as *dogmata* [norms] (see Col 2:14; cf. 2:20), makes them appear as only particular ordinances that stipulate something; they therefore accentuate that facet of the law that, in the sense in which Rom 7:7ff understands it, as well as Gal 3 and 4 and Col 2, is

---

26 Zerwick, *Ephesians*, 61.

27 "The Christian community has a universal openness. In it, the Jews and the 'Nations' are fully reconciled. Together, 'the one and the other' obtain through Christ ('through him') access 'to the Father,' 'in one Spirit' (2:18)." Vanhoye, "Salut universel," 827.

28 Cf. Col 3:4: "Christ who is our life."

29 Schlier, *Efesios*, 165.

30 "The law that is no longer Torah, God's instructions for life, but imperatives and exigencies, of a legalistic and casuistic nature, that are imposed by the powers of the world." Schlier, *Efesios*, 174. Recent approaches to Paul interpret the Law in this narrower sense as referring to "halakhic rulings used to bolster Jewish identity at the expense of inclusion of the Gentiles." Gillman, "Ephesians," 1675. Regarding the observance of the Law as a distinguishing characteristic of Jews in the Roman Empire, and especially in Ephesus, see Thielman, *Ephesians*, 166.

the means of the powers and of sin, the means that takes away sin and the curse of death. Obviously, it is the Jewish law or the human law in general that disturbs and inverts the meaning of the divine instructions, of the Torah, and even goes to the point of abusing them, and does not presuppose grace but only provokes the desire for human implementations. If this casuistic and legalistic law is destroyed—according to the apostle—the "enmity" is then eliminated.[31]

Christ has destroyed the law, which, as a "barrier," separated Israel from the gentiles and therefore constituted a separation between God and human beings.[32] From Israel and the gentiles, a new creation in Christ, characterized by its unity, has thus been created: "*one* new man" (v. 15).[33] The cross of Christ has achieved reconciliation (v. 16); hence peace is now announced, not only for those who are near (the Jews), but also for those who are far away (all the nations: v. 17). A unique fulfillment of the Scripture's prophecy is thus achieved (cf. Isa 57:19). Verse 18 shows, finally, the Trinitarian dimension of this cosmic event: through Christ we human beings have all gained, in the one Spirit, access to the Father.

Then Paul expounds on the joyful consequences of this new situation:

So then you are no longer strangers and sojourners, but you are fellow citizens with the saints and members of the household of God, built upon

---

31 Schlier, *Efesios*, 165. In the letter to the Romans, Paul specifies this thought. As the wife is no longer joined to the husband after his death and is therefore free to remarry, the law takes possession of man while he lives, but when he dies, he is no longer subject to it; the Christian has died with Christ Jesus, so that he is no longer joined to the law, but he lives under grace (Rom 7:1–4; cf. Gal 2:19). This, however, does not prevent an elevated conception of the law as the collection of instructions that reach their ultimate fulfillment in charity; cf. Rom 13:9; 1 Cor 7:19. Romans 3:21, in a single verse, shows us the two meanings of the law: "the righteousness of God has been manifested apart from the law" (where *law* refers to a collection of norms), but "the law and the prophets bear witness to it" (where *law* refers to the revelation of God). Cf. Filippo Belli, "'Testimoniada por la ley y los profetas'. Rom 3,21: Pablo y las Escrituras," *RevAg* 43 (2002): 413–26.

32 "Through no fault of its own, the Mosaic law's introduction increased the trespass and only made rebellion against God worse (Rom. 5:20; 7:11–12). With its removal, the way was clear for the union of Jewish and Gentile believers in Christ (Eph. 2:15) and the Spirit (v. 16), and for the reconciliation between all humanity, across ethnic lines, to God (vv. 16–18)." Thielman, *Ephesians*, 163. Cf. Schlier, *Efesios*, 170; Zerwick, *Ephesians*, 64–65.

33 "The expression . . . is, in itself, quite surprising. . . . We would expect to be told: . . . one new people. . . . Here, by speaking thus, he mentions . . . Adam by name and we would have to put it in quotation marks, according to the mind of the apostle." Schlier, *Efesios*, 175.

the foundation of the apostles and prophets, Christ Jesus himself being the cornerstone, in whom the whole structure is joined together and grows into a holy temple in the Lord; in whom you also are built into it for a dwelling place of God in the Spirit. (Eph 2:19–22)

The gentiles, who before were deprived of citizenship in Israel (Eph 2:12), are now "fellow citizens" (v. 19); hence they participate in the citizenship of the renewed Israel. Those who were strangers and sojourners before are now members of full right in the people of the saints.[34] And they are integrated into this new temple, which, consolidated on the foundations of the eschatological Israel, has Christ as its principle of cohesion: they are "co-built" (v. 22). In this way there is no longer any distinction. Both those who come from Judaism and those who come from a gentile background form a single and inseparable temple of God. The Church is, therefore, the one people consisting of those who are saved by Christ, both Jews and gentiles. However, "the Mosaic law was still authoritative Scripture within the new people of God, but in a different way than it had been for Israel. It revealed the character of God, the nature of humanity, and the centrality of faith to a right relationship with God, but its commandments no longer governed the behavior of God's people without first passing through the filter of the gospel."[35]

C.5. Justification by Faith and Charity

According to St. Paul's most characteristic doctrine (amply exhibited in the letters to the Galatians and the Romans), human beings are not justified before God by submitting to the law of Moses and observing its precepts. What makes human beings agreeable to God is their adherence to Jesus Christ through faith: "But now the righteousness of God has been manifested apart from law, although the law and the prophets bear witness to it, the righteousness of God through faith in Jesus Christ for all who believe. For

---

34 "We have no longer any idea now of the pride with which the man of antiquity felt himself as 'citizen' of his tiny city-state. It meant freedom, protection of law, the right to vote on all matters of public interest, responsibility with others for a great and sacred inheritance. That made life rich and worthwhile for the citizen of the ancient state." Zerwick, *Ephesians*, 69.

35 Thielman, *Ephesians*, 170.

there is no distinction.... For we hold that a man is justified by faith apart from works of law" (Rom 3:21–22, 28).

To universal sin, God responds with universal salvation, without ethnic differences (3:22). "All" have sinned (3:23), both gentiles (Rom 1) and Jews (Rom 2–3); and "all" are gratuitously justified by the grace of God, by virtue of redemption in Christ Jesus (3:24). This new "economy of salvation" makes possible the Church's openness to non-Jews. Before, the proselytes had to make the sign of the covenant in their flesh in order to benefit from it. Now a more profound rite is asked of them: baptism, which brings to fulfillment the "circumcision of the heart" that already constituted the Old Testament ideal.[36] Justification by faith excludes all particularism, so that Israel can no longer be opposed to the pagan world; both groups receive justification in the same way, gratuitously, with an identical act of faith (Rom 3:20–23). Religious opposition between the Jew and the Greek is resolved in a superior unity.[37]

However—just as the Church's later history will demonstrate—by not being required to submit to a series of practices that characterize the Jewish people, the gentiles can adhere to the faith while conserving their own culture, purified by the gospel. This makes it possible for human beings of all races and all times to receive justification, the work of the Holy Spirit that at its root consists in adoptive filiation (Rom 8:15; Gal 4:6), and they thus participate in the divine filiation of Jesus.

This has clear practical consequences for one's life: "For in Christ Jesus neither circumcision nor uncircumcision is of any avail, but faith working through love" (Gal 5:6). The gentiles can take as their own God's revelation to Israel (testified to by the Old Testament) without being obligated to submit to all the ritual or legal-type clauses; however, the authenticity of their faith will be verified in their living out of *agape*. For, as Paul teaches in Galatians and Romans, all of the divine commandments are condensed into charity:

> Owe no one anything, except to love one another; for he who loves his neighbor has fulfilled the law. The commandments, *You shall not commit adultery, You shall not kill, You shall not steal, You shall not covet,* and any

---

36 Deut 10:16; Jer 4:4. Cf. Rom 2:29a: "He is a Jew who is one inwardly, and real circumcision is a matter of the heart, spiritual and not literal."

37 Lyonnet, *La historia de la salvación*, 18.

other commandment, are summed up in this sentence, *You shall love your neighbor as yourself.* Love does no wrong to a neighbor; therefore, love is the fulfilling of the law. (Rom 13:8–10; cf. Gal 5:14)

The gentiles who embrace the faith are called to fulfill the law of God, revealed in the old covenant, but they fulfill it according to its Christian interpretation. Christ, the fullness of revelation, has demonstrated how all those commandments are synthesized in the love of God and love of neighbor (cf. Matt 22:34–40 and parallel passages). The Pauline exhortation (*paraklēsis*), which is centered on *agape*, is explained by this fact.[38] The Christians coming from a gentile background will need to be guided, then, by that *agape* that is ultimately a gift from God that "has been poured into our hearts through the Holy Spirit who has been given to us" (Rom 5:5).

The work of Christ, as understood and preached by Paul, is accessible to all human beings; for in order to be justified by God the decisive factor is faith in Christ, and in order to please him the only requirement is charity. The anthropological and moral doctrine of Paul is in accordance with the universality of salvation brought by Jesus.

C.6. Conclusion: The Gentiles, a Pleasing Offering to God

In chapter 15 of the letter to the Romans, Paul refers in the following way to his own understanding of the vocation he received: "But on some points I have written to you very boldly by way of reminder, because of the grace given me by God to be a minister of Christ Jesus to the gentiles in the priestly service of the gospel of God, so that the offering of the gentiles may be acceptable, sanctified by the Holy Spirit" (Rom 15:15–16). In liturgical language, Paul describes the new situation of the gentiles as a pleasing "offering" that is "sanctified by the Holy Spirit." Those who before were far from God now have intimate access to God and have been made fully acceptable to the Lord. The work of Christ, in whom Jews and gentiles have overcome their difference in order to enter into communion with the Father, has transformed all those who in the past were "by nature children of wrath" (Eph 2:3) into an

---

38 Luis Sánchez-Navarro, "Cristo y la paraclesis en Pablo," in *Pablo y Cristo. La centralidad de Cristo en el pensamiento de san Pablo*, ed. Luis Sánchez-Navarro, CMat 5 (Madrid: San Dámaso, 2009), 177–83.

offering that pleases God. The "priestly service of the gospel of God" has thus achieved its full efficacy. But what is the situation, then, of historical Israel? Paul posed this question earlier in the same letter to the Romans.

D. THE SITUATION OF ISRAEL: BETWEEN SORROW AND HOPE (ROM 9–11)

The reality of justification through faith in Christ leads one to ask about the current status of the chosen people, of which only a small portion in Paul's time had believed while the majority remained hostile to Christianity. The apostle dedicates three chapters of the letter to the Romans to this situation. In his argumentation, and after a poignant overture (the current situation of Israel is all the more poignant given its greater prerogatives: Rom 9:1–5), he proceeds in three phases:

a) First, the situation does not imply a failure of the word of God—that is, of God himself (Rom 9:6–29). On the contrary, this result was already predicted in Scripture.[39] Hence, in order to show the conformity of the call to the gentiles with God's plan, Paul cites Hosea 2:25 ("Those who were not my people I will call 'my people,' and her who was not beloved I will call 'my beloved'": Rom 9:25) and Hosea 2:1 ("And in the very place where it was said to them, 'You are not my people,' they will be called 'sons of the living God'": Rom 9:26).[40] And in order to justify the faith in Jesus of only a reduced number of Jews, he cites two texts of Isaiah characterized by the theme of the "remnant of Israel": Isaiah 10:22–23 ("Though the number of the sons of Israel be as the sand of the sea, only a remnant of them will be saved; for the Lord will execute his sentence upon the earth with rigor and dispatch": Rom 9:27–28)[41] and Isaiah 1:9 ("If the Lord of

---

39 "He [God] even makes use of human indocility to accomplish his ends (9:14–24)." Joseph A. Fitzmyer, "Letter to the Romans," in *NJBC*, 857.

40 "In the original text the words refer to God's restoration of the ten tribes of Israel after they have committed 'adultery' (=idolatry) and ceased to be his people. Hosea promised their restoration, but for Paul the words refer to the Gentiles." Fitzmyer, "Romans," 858.

41 "The words were used originally by Isaiah of the Assyrian captivity; Paul applies them to the Jews called to accept Christ and to the remnant that did so." Fitzmyer, "Romans," 858. The RSV translation is "only a remnant," but the Greek text does not say "only."

hosts had not left us children,[42] we would have fared like Sodom and been made like Gomorrah": Rom 9:29).

b) Next, Paul explains why Israel has remained in this tragic situation (9:30–10:21). It is owing to the incredulity and sin of Israel—which is also amply attested in Scripture. Israel wanted to base its righteousness on its own works, by which it closed itself off to the revelation of God in Jesus Christ (9:30–33). Since these Jews have not believed in Jesus, they cannot obtain from him their righteousness; their incredulity has made them incapable of recognizing God's plan fulfilled in Jesus (cf. 10:18–21).

> His argument proceeds in four steps. (1) Israel has preferred its own way of uprightness to that of God (9:31–33). (2) Paul expresses his sorrow that Israel has failed to recognize that Christ is the end of the Law and that uprightness been made attainable through him (10:1–4). (3) The old way of attaining uprightness was difficult, whereas the new way is easy, within the reach of all and announced to all, as Scripture shows (10:5–13). (4) Israel has not taken advantage of this opportunity offered by the prophets and the gospel; and so the fault lies with her (10:14–21).[43]

c) This is not, however, the last word on Israel's destiny; the third stage of Paul's exposition (Rom 11:1–36) is dominated by a hopeful vision. God has not rejected his people; the proof of this is that, even though the others hardened their hearts, the "remnant"—to which the apostle belongs—has indeed believed (11:1–10). The incredulity of Israel is only partial.[44] It is also only temporary, and not definitive (11:11–24); Paul affirms that if God has permitted it, he has done so in order to draw out a greater benefit from it all, not only for the Jews but for all humanity (vv. 11–15). With audacious hope he upholds, "Now if their trespass means riches for the world, and if their failure means riches for the Gentiles, how much more will their full

---

42 The term in Hebrew is "a survivor" (*śārîd*). The Septuagint translates it as *sperma*, interpreting it as "seed." This allows Paul to frame the first phase of his argument (cf. *sperma* in 9:7–8) and may recall the theme of Jesus as offspring (Gal 3:16).

43 Fitzmyer, "Romans," 858.

44 Cf. Fitzmyer, "Romans," 860.

inclusion mean!" (v. 12); "For if their rejection means the reconciliation of the world, what will their acceptance mean but life from the dead?" (v. 15). Paul implies that the present situation of the chosen people is provisional.[45] Then, with the image of the olive tree and the wild olive shoot (vv. 16–24), he exhorts the Christians of pagan origin not to become conceited about their situation, because not in vain are they benefitting from the holy root that has engendered the Jews who do not believe in Jesus; the end commensurate with this conceit would be even more pitiful. And, moreover, God can regraft the Jews who end up believing into the olive plant that is connatural to them.[46]

In this third stage, we then find a section in which Paul makes explicit the *mystērion*, the hidden plan of God. God is going to show mercy to all, especially to the Jews (11:25–32).[47] On the one hand, Paul shows how Israel's refusal to recognize Jesus as Messiah has had a paradoxical positive effect in terms of pagans accepting the Christian faith.[48] On the other, once "the full number of the Gentiles come in" to the Church (v. 25), "all Israel will be

---

45 See Paul Beauchamp, "Israele e le nazioni fuori e dentro la Chiesa: Lettura di Romani 9–11," in *Stili di compimento. Lo Spirito e la lettera nelle Scritture* (Assisi: Citadella, 2007), 194.

46   What he means seems clear: that [the gentile believers] should feel immense respect not only for the branches that are in their own place [the Jewish remnant] and are bringing forth the fruits belonging to the tree (9:4 taught us to see a great continuity between the promises and their fulfillment!), but also for the branches broken off. As if to say that God does not want them to dry up (another paradox!) but that they are always at the point of being regrafted (cf. 11:23). For this reason, even though Paul has enthusiastically given himself to his mission as apostle to the gentiles (v. 13b; cf. 1:5), he never loses sight of the Jewish People (11:14).

Jordi Sánchez Bosch, *Maestro de los pueblos: Una teología de Pablo, el apóstol* (Estella, Spain: Verbo Divino, 2007), 426.

47 The *mystērion* "ultimately says that Israel's hardening does not preclude its salvation and is instead scandalously directed toward the salvation of the Gentiles." Filippo Belli, *Argumentation and Use of Scripture in Romans 9–11*, AnBib 183 (Rome: Gregorian & Biblical Press, 2010), 397; cf. 386–405: "The Final Proof: The Revelation of the 'Mystery.'"

48 Israel's infidelity "is providential, that is, ordered to the salvation of all; without this infidelity, perhaps the masses of pagans would not have converted; and if the small number of those converted from Judaism made Paul's apostolate so difficult, . . . what would have happened if Israel had converted *en masse*? With good reason Paul can write that the pagans 'have received mercy because of [the Jews'] disobedience' (Rom 11:30)." Lyonnet, *La historia de la salvación*, 25. Cf. Beauchamp, "Israele e le nazioni," 200.

saved" (v. 26). In view of the revealed *mystērion*, Paul also finds support in
Scripture (Isa 59:20–21 and 27:9; Rom 11:27).[49] The underlying reason is the
gifts received from God: "For the gifts and the call from God are irrevocable"
(v. 29).

> In Isaiah's visions [59:20–21; 27:9], the ultimate restoration of Israel is the
> gracious work of their God, who comes in person to remove their sins
> and reconcile them to himself. Like the prophet, Paul trusts with absolute
> confidence in the mercy and faithfulness of God that "the rest" of Israel
> (Rom 11:7) will one day be rescued from their unbelief (Rom 11:20, 23).
> In that day, "all Israel" will embrace their God, who has acted in Christ for
> their deliverance as well as for the salvation of the gentiles.[50]

The chapter concludes with a doxology (11:33–36) in which Paul proclaims—again supporting himself with Scripture—how unfathomable is
God's wisdom, which is the basis of this paradoxical but consoling salvific
plan: the entrance of the gentiles into the Church is a necessary prelude to
the conversion of the chosen people.[51] Paul's desire to advance the definitive salvation of his people moves him to evangelize all the nations: "For if I
preach the gospel, that gives me no ground for boasting. For necessity is laid
upon me. Woe to me if I do not preach the gospel!" (1 Cor 9:16).[52]

---

49 Cf. Rom 15:8–9.

> Let us highlight: "From Zion . . . from Jacob . . . with them" [11:26–27], insofar as "to
> them belong . . . the covenants" (Rom 9:4), the Old and the New. The gentiles will
> also enter into it, but with the difference that we go from something being given
> through "faithfulness" (Rom 15:8) to something being given through "mercy" (Rom
> 15:9a). It will be the Jews who will praise God in the midst of all peoples (Rom
> 15:9b) and, immediately afterwards, invite the nations to rejoice with the people
> of God (15:10).

Sánchez Bosch, *Maestro de los pueblos*, 427.

50 J. Ross Wagner, "Isaiah in Romans and Galatians," in *Isaiah in the New Testament*, ed. S.
Moyise and M. J. J. Menken, NTSI (London: T&T Clark, 2005), 126.

51 "It is true that Paul is the apostle to the pagans, but if he accepts this unexpected 'glory' of
leading such a great number of idolaters to the true God and his righteousness, it is . . . for
the Jews! It is because the Jews are 'pinched' by seeing the pagans transformed; even though
the pagans were sinners, they now live righteously." Beauchamp, "Israele e le nazioni," 192.

52 "It is a bit shocking that the apostle to the Gentiles seems to have seen the conversion of
the Gentiles, not as an end in itself, but as a halfway step toward the conversion of Israel."
Raymond E. Brown, *An Introduction to the New Testament*, ABRL (New York: Doubleday,
1997), 571.

"In this sense, the urgency of evangelization in the apostolic era was predicated not so much on the necessity for each individual to acquire knowledge of the gospel in order to attain salvation, but rather on this grand conception of history: if the world was to arrive at its destiny, the gospel had to be brought to all nations."[53] In summary, Israel's present situation is sorrowful but provisional.[54] Paul's faith is transformed into a declaration of hope; the people of the covenant will benefit from the Lord's fulfillment of that covenant. The people as a whole will thus participate in the salvation of Jesus Christ; moreover, represented in that "remnant" of which Paul is part, the chosen people is already receiving the first fruits of that definitive fulfillment. Paul discovers this, in part due to his faith-driven view of the present moment. Paul sees the salvation of the gentiles, who are already benefiting from the covenant established by God with the chosen people, as the prelude to the salvation of "all Israel" (11:26), announced by the prophets.[55] The universalism of the gospel will not mean the dissolution of Israel, but rather the fullness of salvation for it; the apostle affirms that God in his fidelity will fulfill all his promises to Israel, through the chosen people's believing acceptance of Jesus the Messiah.[56] This is because his gospel "is the power of God for salvation to every one who has faith, to the Jew first and also to the Greek" (Rom 1:16); "there is no distinction between Jew and Greek; the same Lord is Lord of all and bestows his riches upon all who call upon him" (10:12).

53 Joseph Ratzinger (Benedict XVI), *Jesus of Nazareth: Holy Week: From the Entrance into Jerusalem to the Resurrection*, trans. Philip J. Whitmore (San Francisco: Ignatius Press, 2011), 44; see 41–45: "The Times of the Gentiles."

54 It is therefore out of place to claim for the current moment "two ways of salvation": that of the covenant of Israel and that of the new covenant. The hope of Paul, who loves and thus respects these branches that are cut off from the good olive plant, is based on the chosen people's eschatological orientation towards Christ. "According to Gal 3:15–18, 29, after the coming of Christ, the only way to relate authentically to the covenant with Abraham is to adhere to Christ." Vanhoye, "Salut universel," 821.

55 "In this way Paul not only confirms Israel's election, which remains, but also the still-pending fulfillment of the prophetic promises in relation to the final restoration of Israel and the resulting return of 'all Israel' (that is, of the 'house of Israel' and of the 'house of Judah') to YHWH." Jacob Thiessen, *Gott hat Israel nicht verstoßen: Biblisch-exegetische Perspektiven in der Verhältnisbestimmung von Israel, Judentum und Gemeinde Jesu*, EDIS 3 (Frankfurt am Main: Peter Lang, 2010), 195.

56 Thiessen, *Gott hat Israel nicht verstoßen*, 100.

E. CONCLUSION

The letters of Paul, a Jew and apostle to the gentiles, confirm the gospel doctrine about the universalism of Christ's mission. By his passion the Lord has united those who were previously separated; in the new salvific system, the only requirement for achieving justification is "faith working through love" (Gal 5:6). With his apostolic ministry and the doctrine that filters through his letters, Saint Paul collaborated powerfully in the universal diffusion of the gospel, that is, in the growth of the Catholic Church. This, however, does not deprive the people of Israel of their salvific relevance. Not only has Israel made it possible for salvation to reach all nations, but even the hardened part of Israel is called to be eschatologically grafted back into salvation, as the sign of the definitive fulfillment of God's plan.

CHAPTER SEVEN

Other Voices
of the New Testament

After our tour through the great *corpora* of the New Testament (the synoptic, Johannine, and Pauline traditions), we now direct our attention to some New Testament writings that, though related to those traditions, have their own personality: the letter to the Hebrews (belonging to the Pauline *corpus*) and the Book of Revelation (belonging to the Johannine tradition). Both are marked by their profound rootedness in Israel's Scriptures and, at the same time, by a very distinctive teaching.

A. THE LETTER TO THE HEBREWS

This writing is unique in the New Testament for its literary form (a synagogal homily[1]) and for its central theme: the priesthood of Christ. It thus represents a valuable testimony of the gospel as it was lived by the first Christian communities.

If all the New Testament writings are rooted in Israel's Scriptures, then the letter to the Hebrews is so rooted in a special way; the whole letter constitutes an updated interpretation, in light of the Risen Jesus, of Ps 110:4 ("You are a priest for ever according to the order of Melchizedek"). It is the only New Testament writing that explicitly speaks of Jesus as priest; all of the theological categories that are applied come from the Old Testament. It

---

1 This literally means a "word of exhortation" (*logos paraklēseōs*: Heb 13:22; cf. Acts 13:15).

is therefore a writing with a strong Judeo-Christian flavor.[2] A first reading allows us to verify, moreover, that in this letter the term *ethnos* (nation) does not appear, nor does any derivation of it; as such, the letter does not treat the "gentiles." All these elements ultimately make this book, in a certain way, the most "Old Testament book" of the New Testament. What role, then, does the universal dimension of salvation play?

A.1. The Beginning of the Letter

The preamble of Hebrews places the Christ event in a perspective of the broadest scope: "but in these last days he has spoken to us by a Son, whom he appointed the heir of all things, through whom also he created the ages" (Heb 1:2). It is crystal clear that the fruit of Jesus' passion is universal ("heir of all things"). The allusion to the work of creation (through Christ) confirms this, as creation is a quintessentially universal theme. The letter continues to develop along the same lines ("upholding the universe by the word of his power": 1:3).

This vision is confirmed later, still in the initial part of the letter, by the exegesis of Ps 8:6 ("you have put all things under his feet"): "Now in putting everything in subjection to him, he left nothing outside his control" (Heb 2:8). And the following verse affirms that Jesus tasted death "for every one" (Heb 2:9). A little later we are told that Jesus suffered in order to "deliver those who through fear of death were subject to lifelong bondage" (2:15), that is, all human beings. Hence, even though the author then clarifies that "surely it is not with angels that he is concerned but with the descendants of Abraham" (2:16) and speaks of "expiation for the sins of the people" (2:17)—thus placing Christ's work in a special relationship with Israel—the horizon on which he

---

2 Hence its title, "To the Hebrews." "According to the ancient Church's understanding, the expression generally refers to the Jewish Christians of Palestine." Knut Backhaus, *Der sprechende Gott: Gesammelte Studien zum Hebräerbrief*, WUNT 240 (Tübingen: Mohr Siebeck, 2009), 195 n. 1. This does not rule out that the addressees of the letter also included gentile Christians (as in fact occurred in the ancient Church in practically all the Christian communities). In any case, because there is no explicit data in the letter, the question remains open: "The recipients may have been of Jewish origin, but nothing precludes their being gentiles." Harold W. Attridge, *Essays on John and Hebrews*, WUNT 264 (Tübingen: Mohr Siebeck, 2010), 281. Cf. Franco Manzi, *Carta a los Hebreos*, CBJer.NT 6 (Bilbao: Desclée de Brouwer, 2005), 14–15.

situates that work goes beyond the chosen people. Therefore, already in the traditional Christological exposition with which he opens his writing, the author of this letter demonstrates that the salvation accomplished by Jesus has creation itself as its horizon; that is, it is extended to all human beings.[3] The high priesthood of the merciful and faithful Jesus (2:18) is therefore something new.

A.2. A New Priesthood

The main message of the letter is, indeed, that Jesus is the High Priest, but also that his priesthood is of a radically new form. It derives from the biblical model that allows us to understand it: Melchizedek (Heb 5:6, 10). In effect, Melchizedek is a mysterious person in the Old Testament; his presence in Israel's Scriptures is confined to three verses of the Torah (Gen 14:18–20) and Psalm 110, already cited. Despite apparently being a non-Hebrew, he is presented as the "king of Salem" and "priest of God Most High." This is thus a matter of a priesthood that is antecedent to that of Aaron; Melchizedek is, in fact, the first priest (*kōhēn*) mentioned by the Torah. He is, however, first not only in time, but also in dignity; the fact that he blesses Abraham, who also gives him a tithe, is an implicit recognition of Melchizedek's superiority. Thus, even before recounting the institution of the Levitical priesthood, the Old Testament places before us the image of a different and superior priesthood.[4] Moreover, the author insists that Melchizedek does not have a genealogy (Heb 7:3); he is not said to belong to any ethnic entity. Consequently, the priesthood of Christ will be of a different order than the Levitical one.

This new priesthood corresponds to the new covenant, announced by Jeremiah (Jer 31:31–34; Heb 8:8–12). It also corresponds to a new sanctuary (cf. 8:2), a "tent" that is no longer the holy of holies of the temple in Jerusalem, constructed with stone (cf. 9:3, 6–7), but one that has been directly created

---

3 For a concentric structure of Hebrews, cf. Albert Vanhoye, *The Letter to the Hebrews: A New Commentary*, trans. Leo Arnold (New York: Paulist, 2015), 17–20. After the introduction (1:1–4), the letter's structure is articulated in five major sections: (I) Brief Exposition of Traditional Christology (1:5–2:18); (II) First Exposition of Sacerdotal Christology: Essential Aspects (3:1–5:10); (III) Second Exposition of Sacerdotal Christology: Specific Features (5:11–10:39); (IV) Examples of Faith and Exhortation to Persevere (11:1–12:13); and (V) Exhortation: Sanctity and Peace (12:14–13:18).

4 Cf. Vanhoye, *Hebrews*, 119.

by God (8:2), "not made with hands, that is, not of this creation" (9:11). The new "tent" is the flesh of the Risen Jesus; through his body and his blood (9:12) he entered into the new sanctuary: heaven (9:24), a universal reality par excellence.[5] Hence, the sacrifice offered "once for all" (7:27; 9:12; 10:10), has become the cause of salvation for "those who draw near to God through him" (7:25). In Hebrews, it is understood that this salvation is never conditional upon one's belonging to the chosen people or upon observance of the Torah; the exhortations to believe, which demarcate the letter and are condensed especially in chapter 11, point to faith as the only condition for benefiting from Christ's priesthood.

A.3. Hebrews: A Theology of Substitution?

The novelty wrought by the paschal mystery of Christ is so important that it is revealed as the origin of a *new* covenant. Does this covenant substitute for the old covenant, so that the old can be considered definitively abolished? It seems that one could draw this conclusion from a fundamental passage of the letter: the prophecy of the new covenant (Jer 31:31–34), cited in its very center. It is the most extensive Old Testament citation of the whole letter (Heb 8:8–12).

Let us begin by noting the obvious: it is clear that Israel's cultic regimen is substantially abrogated in the Church; the meticulously described sacrifices in the Torah are no longer offered.[6] Even the temple is considered unnecessary.[7] But is this equivalent to declaring that the old covenant has expired?

---

5 "The tent that is 'not of this creation'. . . can only be the body of the glorified Christ, a new creation, thanks to which Christ has entered into the sanctuary of God, that is to say into the intimacy of God." Vanhoye, *Hebrews*, 145. This tent is greater because "the glorified body of Christ . . . receives all believers, who become his 'members' (1 Cor 12:27; Eph 5:30); the faithful are 'sharers of Christ' (Heb 3:14); they are 'his house' (Heb 3:6)." Vanhoye, *Hebrews*, 146.

6 "If something has been 'substituted,' it is the Levitical sacrifice of animals (which also occurred, for another reason and in another way, in Judaism at that time)." Backhaus, *Der sprechende Gott*, 200.

7 See in this regard Ratzinger, *Holy Week*, 2:28–41: "The End of the Temple." Despite the fact that the Old Testament sacrifices have been abrogated, however, they are still present in the quintessential sacrifice of the New Testament: the Eucharist. The principal elements of those sacrifices converge in it, while simultaneously taking a radically new form.

In order to orient our response, we must note first of all that the first covenant affirms the limits of Israel's cultic institution and recognizes its symbolic value. The fulfillment of the precepts of the Torah is for nothing if it does not spring from the Israelite's heart. What is important is the circumcision of the heart, without which the circumcision of the flesh is in vain (Deut 10:16; Jer 4:4). Without obedience to God, sacrifices are more than sterile, they are counterproductive (Isa 1).[8] Let us note also that the "new covenant" in Scripture—and consequently in the New Testament—is understood as a new creation, essentially a new Genesis, or return to the beginning.[9] On the other hand, we must note that Hebrews never speaks of a rupture from the covenant, or of Israel's blindness or apostasy.[10] Finally, the fact that the old covenant itself foresees a new one (Jer 31) shows the self-understanding of the Israelite cult as a reality with a clearly provisional component, aiming towards a definitive fulfillment.

The affirmation of this letter is certainly forceful: "In speaking of a new covenant he treats the first as obsolete. And what is becoming obsolete and growing old is ready to vanish away" (Heb 8:13). The whole of the letter, however, gives us the key for understanding these words in their proper measure; they are not about substituting the Jew with the Christian, but rather the fulfillment of what is earthly (imperfect) in the new heavenly (perfect) reality inaugurated by Christ's resurrection. "Conscious of the substantial superiority of the new covenant mediated by Christ, the preacher does not reach the point of declaring the 'first' covenant suppressed. He ends, however, by attributing to God himself [the subject of the verb *pepalaiōken* (treat as

---

8 It must be noted that a merely formal living out of Christian worship would also be on the same level as the covenant that Hebrews declares already transcended. Saint Thomas teaches the following:

> There were . . . under the regimen of the old covenant, people who possessed the charity and grace of the Holy Spirit and longed above all for the spiritual and eternal promises by which they were associated with the New Law. Conversely, there exist carnal men under the new covenant, still distanced from the perfection of the New Law; the fear of punishment and certain temporal promises have been necessary, even under the new covenant, to incite them to virtuous works.

Thomas Aquinas, *Summa Theologiae*, I–II, q. 107, a. 1, ad 2; in *CCC*, no. 1964.

9 "The certitude that *the new covenant is more ancient than the old* filled the men who announced it." Beauchamp, *Ley, Profetas, Sabios*, 258.

10 Cf. Backhaus, *Der sprechende Gott*, 200.

obsolete: 8:13)] the judgment about its provisional character."[11] The author, in effect, expresses himself in these terms: "They [the Jewish priests] serve a copy [*hypodeigma*] and shadow [*skia*] of the heavenly sanctuary" (8:5); "the law has but a shadow [*skia*] of the good things to come instead of the true form [*eikōn*] of these realities" (10:1). The relationship between the old and the new covenants is that of a figure or shadow in the presence of the reality; it is therefore a matter of a tight relationship. Hebrews does not speak in a polemical-antithetical perspective, but rather a biblical-antitype one.[12] This does not mean that the new covenant pertains only to the eschatological future;[13] the expiration of the Israelite cult as such is evident for Hebrews.[14] It means, then, that the explanation of mere "substitution" is incorrect because it is insufficient. We find ourselves in the logic of fulfillment, which does not annul promises but rather perpetuates them insofar as they are now fulfilled.

A.4. Conclusion

The unexpected novelty of Christ's priesthood, which has inaugurated a new era in the history of humanity by allowing a new relationship of intimacy with God, does not reduce Israel to irrelevance; in fact, the new covenant prophesied by Jeremiah is "with the house of Israel and with the house of Judah" (Jer 31:31; Heb 8:8). The cultic character—clearly from the Old Testament—of the theme, the vocabulary, and the argument of this writing leads us to turn our eyes constantly towards the worship of the historical Israel and the prefiguration of the new reality. At the same time, Hebrews contains such a radical affirmation of the novelty of Christ that it appears to the Jewish reader as a challenge; it is the Christian challenge of seeing

---

11 Manzi, *Hebreos*, 122.

12 Backhaus, *Der sprechende Gott*, 203. "In Hebrews the question does not turn on the 'infinite superiority of Christianity over Judaism,' but on the infinite superiority of the divine over the earthly, and on the wonder of the closeness of God that is offered as a gift." For a similar perspective, see Alan C. Mitchell, "'A Sacrifice of Praise': Does Hebrews Promote Supersessionism?," in *Reading the Epistle to the Hebrews: A Resource for Students*, ed. Eric F. Mason and Kevin B. McCruden, SBLRBS 66 (Atlanta: SBL, 2011), 251–67.

13 As Jesper Svartvik maintains in "Leggere la Lettera agli Ebrei senza presupporre la teologia della sostituzione," in *Gesù Cristo e il popolo ebraico: Interrogativi per la teologia di oggi*, ed. Philip A. Cunningham et al., BibDial 5 (Rome: Gregorian & Biblical Press, 2012), 129–47.

14 See in this regard Vanhoye, "Salut universel," 829–34.

in Jesus the "truth" of the ancient "figures"—a "truth" whose fruits are not limited to Israel but reach the entire creation, that is, all human beings.[15] The continued existence of the Jerusalem temple at the time in which the letter was written manifested, then, the tension between the temple of stone and the new "tent," the Risen Christ.[16] This same tension continues to exist today between the Israel of the flesh and the Church—a tension that is called to be resolved not by a key of substitution but of fulfillment.

B. THE REVELATION TO JOHN

The book that closes the Christian Bible presents to us a grandiose vision of the history of salvation and of the life of the Church. This history is wrapped in great cosmic events and decisive confrontations between the forces of good and those of evil; the paradoxical protagonist is a lamb, an animal that is symbolic of fragility and meekness. It is, however, a very unique lamb because, though it has been slain, it is standing (Rev 5:6) and it has the strength of the "Lion of the tribe of Judah" (5:5). The true protagonist of history, hidden behind this symbol, is Jesus, who after his passion lives resurrected and glorious.

B.1. The Addressees of the Book of Revelation

This prophetic book is directed to "the seven churches of Asia" (Rev 1:11).[17] Its addressees are therefore the Christian residents in the Roman province of Asia Minor, a region of elevated Hellenistic culture in which incipient Christianity took root in a powerful way (as the Pauline and Johannine traditions attest).[18] The book is, we might say, a "circular" letter. At the same time, it is not limited to the churches enunciated, as the numerical symbolism (so important in Revelation) suggests: "seven" is in Scripture a symbolic

15 "For Christ has entered, not into a sanctuary made with hands, a copy [antitypos] of the true one [alēthinos], but into heaven itself, now to appear in the presence of God on our behalf" (Heb 9:24). Cf. Heb 8:2: "the true tent."

16 Heb 5:1; 8:3; 9:7, 25. Cf. Vanhoye, Hebrews, 14–15.

17 Ephesus, Smyrna, Pergamum, Thyatira, Sardis, Philadelphia, and Laodicea.

18 See in this regard Klemens Stock, La última palabra es de Dios: El Apocalipsis como Buena Noticia (Madrid: San Pablo, 2005), 12–17.

expression of totality, of plenitude. Therefore, by addressing the letter to seven churches, the author symbolically "sends" it to all the churches of that time, or to the whole Church. This was already noted in the Muratorian Fragment: "John, even though he writes to seven churches in Revelation, nevertheless speaks to all."[19]

B.2. A Universal Horizon

The Old Testament has such a massive presence in the Book of Revelation that one can say that this book is in a certain way a rewriting of the Old Testament in light of Christ resurrected.[20] This could perhaps lead one to think that the perspective of this book is particular, that it is centered on Israel, but nothing could be further from reality. The key to reading the Old Testament is the eschatological messianic fulfillment in Jesus Christ.[21] This fulfillment exceeds the limits of Israel in order to affect all of creation.

The perspective that dominates the whole book is a universal one. Already from the beginning Jesus is presented as the "ruler of kings on earth" (Rev 1:5), the one whom "every eye will see" (1:7). His self-designation as "the Alpha and the Omega, the first and the last, the beginning and the end" (22:13; cf. 1:8) places him in relation with the entire creation, indicating his presence and activity within it.[22] The fact that one of the levels that is constant in the narrative is "heaven" (see, for example, chapter 4) implies a universal scope for the Lamb's action. This is confirmed by the effects of that action, as proclaimed by the celestial beings: "by your blood you ransomed men for God

19 In *Enquiridion bíblico. Documentos de la Iglesia sobre la Sagrada Escritura*, ed. Carlos Granados and Luis Sánchez-Navarro (Madrid: BAC, 2010), no. 4. "The fact that the list contains seven Churches should not surprise anyone. . . . This number undoubtedly signifies totality and ecumenism." Pierre Prigent, *Commentary on the Apocalypse of St. John* (Tübingen: Mohr Siebeck, 2001), 131.

20 More than eight hundred references to the Old Testament are found in Revelation: Ugo Vanni, *Apocalisse e Antico Testamento: Una sinossi*, 2nd ed. (Rome: Pontificio Istituto Biblico, 1987).

21 "The novelty of the Book of Revelation is precisely in the author's rereading of Scripture; in light of the revelation offered by Christ, he 'rewrites' the ancient texts, placing them in a new context and opening them up for a full understanding of the divine plan of salvation." Ricardo A. Pérez Márquez, *L'Antico Testamento nell'Apocalisse: Storia della ricerca, bilancio e prospettive* (Assisi: Cittadella, 2010), 448.

22 Hermann Lichtenberger, *Die Apokalypse*, TKNT 23 (Stuttgart: Kohlhammer, 2014), 67.

from every tribe and tongue and people and nation" (5:9); this quadruple expression appears with slight variations at various moments in the book, so much so that it constitutes one of its literary characteristics (5:9; 7:9; 10:11; 11:9; 13:7; 14:6; 17:15). The salvation brought by Christ affects all human beings, independently of their ethnic or cultural origin.[23] Likewise, as a consequence of his redemptive action, the "seven spirits of God" (that is, the plenitude of the Spirit) have been sent to "all the earth" (5:6). In principle, no human being is denied this gift.[24]

The calamities that run throughout the book are also universal; hence the horsemen of chapter 6 have power to take away peace from the earth (the red horse) or to damage a quarter part of the earth (the green horse). Worthy of special mention are the cosmic catastrophes that mark the narration: the sun that loses its light (6:12; 9:2), the stars that fall from the heavens (6:13; 9:1), the water that suddenly dries up (16:12), etc. It is a matter of symbols that express the radical transformation of the world of human beings by God's presence in history.[25] They thus highlight the universal dimension of the history that is narrated.

B.3. The Number of the Saved

In chapter 7, before the Lamb opens the seventh seal, we have a vision that anticipates the final salvation of all those marked with the seal of God (Rev 7:3). It specifies the number of those marked with the seal as 144,000. This is the result of squaring the number of Israel's tribes and in turn multiplying this number by 1,000, which is a symbol of Christ's presence (7:4).[26] Then, in the New Testament's only enumeration of the twelve tribes of Israel,

23 Cf. Prigent, *Apocalypse*, 257.

24 "The Spirit . . . goes out from the Risen Christ and shines forth, in the totality of his manifestations, on all the earth, on all humanity." Ugo Vanni, *Lectura del Apocalipsis: Hermenéutica, exégesis, teología* (Estella, Spain: Verbo Divino, 2005), 203.

25 Cf. Vanni, *Lectura del Apocalipsis*, 44.

26 In a similar way, the wall of the new Jerusalem will be 144 cubits long (Rev 21:17). "The number one thousand expresses, as the largeness of the number and some documentations of its usage suggest, the totality proper to the level of God and the action of Christ." Vanni, *Lectura del Apocalipsis*, 62.

each tribe is allocated 12,000 people destined for salvation (7:5–8).[27] These 144,000 will appear, already triumphant, with the Lamb in Rev 14:1–5. Their salvation is clearly related to their belonging to Israel; however, this fact needs to be interpreted.[28]

Moreover, there are many more than 144,000 who participate in the victory of the Lamb: "a great multitude which no one could number" (7:9). And, in contrast to the preceding, they are characterized by their ethnic plurality: "from every nation, from all tribes and peoples and tongues." With white robes—symbolizing their definitive participation in Christ's victory—they proclaim the salvation already accomplished by God and by the Lamb (7:10). Again, Christ's work brings salvation to all human beings without distinction; the only requirement is making their robes "white in the blood of the Lamb" (7:14), that is, believing in him and giving witness to him with their life. Let us note, all the same, that this fact does not deny the unique relationship of Christ's salvation with Israel, which is manifested in the 144,000 who had been sealed; in fact, the "great multitude" praises the Lamb, that is, the paschal victim.

B.4. The New Jerusalem

John's vision culminates in the new Jerusalem, the city that proceeds from God and that symbolizes universal salvation. In it the tree of life stands out, and it is extraordinarily fruitful (it gives fruit each month). It is also the cause of salvation for the gentiles: "and the leaves of the tree were for the

---

27 Only the tribe of Dan is missing, probably for theological reasons:
> The Old Testament describes the tribe of Dan as idolatrous (Judg 18; 1 Kgs 12:28–30). According to the present form of the *Testaments of the Twelve Patriarchs*, the (angelic) prince of Dan is Satan (*T. Dan* 5:6). A prophecy of judgment is linked to Dan in Jeremiah 8:16–17. These traditions may have been the basis for the later Christian tradition that the Antichrist would come from this tribe (Irenaeus, *Adv. Haer.* 5.30.2).

Adela Y. Collins, "The Book of Revelation," in *JBC XXI*, 1868. Significantly, the author of Revelation wanted to maintain the number twelve; for this reason, he included Manasseh, one of the two sons of Joseph, in the enumeration of the patriarchs.

28 "Membership in the twelve tribes is probably also meant symbolically and not literally. Membership in the Jewish people is not primarily a matter of birth (2:9; 3:9). The use of numbers, however, does suggest that a limited group is meant, not simply all Christians. The identity of this group becomes clearer in 14:1–5." Collins, "Revelation," 1868.

healing of the nations" (22:2). Thus, in the celestial city human beings "from every nation and all tribes and peoples and tongues" find their definitive healing (cf. 7:9).[29] This city is surrounded by a wall, one that is founded on the twelve apostles of the Lamb (21:14). It has twelve gates with twelve names, "the names of the twelve tribes of the sons of Israel" (21:12). "The community of the perfect is the people of God in the perfection of their number and in their fulfillment. The regrouping of this people, whose beginnings find their roots in the history of God with the people of the twelve tribes of Israel and whose continuation is the Church founded upon the twelve apostles, has the communion of the perfect as its goal."[30] The definitive dwelling of God with human beings (cf. 21:3), which is destined for all nations, preserves a fundamental relationship with Israel: in order to enter into this city one must enter through the twelve tribes. Hence, although the salvation symbolized by the city is for all people (which corresponds with the universal horizon that dominates the chapter—"the new heaven and the new earth": 21:1), the reference to the saving mediation of the chosen people remains.[31]

B.5. Conclusion

Our review of John's Revelation, which has been brief and selective, has allowed us to verify that the work of Christ, the immolated but living Lamb, has a universal reach: all human beings are called to benefit from that work. That universal reach, however, does not eliminate the reference to Israel; the fulfillment accomplished by God in Christ is therefore presented in continuity with the salvation to which Scripture testifies, and this fulfillment of the promise does not imply its annulment. The fulfillment contains the promise; moreover, it allows the promise to subsist in a permanent way. Revelation testifies to how, through Israel, all of humanity reaches its definitive dwelling

---

29 "One could not condense better into a single verse (Rev 22:2) the fullness of which we speak: gratuitous forgiveness. Precisely because of its gratuitousness, it goes beyond the borders of Israel in favor of the nations, while respecting the particularity of Jerusalem." Yves Simoens, *Apocalisse di Giovanni, Apocalisse di Gesù Cristo: Una traduzione e un'interpretazione* (Bologna: Dehoniane, 2010), 251–52.

30 Stock, *La última palabra es de Dios*, 191.

31 "The people of the twelve tribes, as the definitive salvific community, has a part in the New Jerusalem." Lichtenberger, *Apokalypse*, 264.

in that city in which—recalling the Old Testament promises (Isa 25:8)—God "will wipe away every tear from their eyes, and death shall be no more, neither shall there be mourning nor crying nor pain any more, for the former things have passed away" (Rev 21:4).

Conclusions
and Perspectives

Our tour through the principal testimonies of the New Testament, a tour founded on the open horizon of the Old Testament, has allowed us to describe how universalism is a fundamental element of the gospel of Jesus Christ. This has important consequences on multiple levels. I will now point out some relevant aspects that allow us to conclude this study and at the same time point us towards a new beginning.

A. FROM THE OLD TESTAMENT TO THE NEW TESTAMENT

The Old Testament, as we have verified, is not a reality closed in on itself; on the contrary, it is constitutively open, in its entirety and in each one of its great parts. Many passages, however, also explicitly present a universal horizon for the salvation that God wants to reveal. Israel, Abraham's progeny, does not exist for itself alone but to be converted into a "light for the nations," just as is affirmed of the Servant of YHWH; God the creator of everything is the God who wants to save everyone. The New Testament writings are connected to this fundamental teaching, and they develop it; through the new reality of Jesus Christ, God fulfills the expectations contained in the Tanak. The Risen Christ's commandment, the universal preaching of the gospel, shows God's fidelity to his plan to offer salvation to all human beings.

The New Testament gives a consistent testimony on all this, from its first page (Matt 1) to its last (Rev 22). The writings we have studied, belonging to the principal traditions of the New Testament (synoptic, Pauline, Johannine), have presented us with a consistent message: in Jesus the Messiah, God's promises and Israel's expectations are definitively fulfilled. The relevance of the chosen people is beyond doubt; it is not diluted in this new reality, but on the contrary, it reaches its greatest fulfillment. Yet Christ's resurrection has profoundly affected the nature of this people, which now achieves its true identity by being open to all people. In Jesus, Israel becomes what it was called to be from the beginning.

B. JESUS, "LIGHT OF THE NATIONS" AND FULFILLMENT OF ISRAEL

According to what Matthew suggests, the manifestation of Jesus to Israel means a true dawn with universal resonances; "Galilee of the Gentiles" (Matt 4:15) thus becomes a setting that anticipates Jesus, the son of Abraham (Matt 1:1), fulfilling the promise made to the patriarch: "and by your descendants shall all the nations of the earth bless themselves" (Gen 22:18). Jesus has not done this outside of Israel, but precisely in assuming the chosen people's mission in his own person as the Servant and in calling the reconstituted Israel (the Twelve) in order to develop this mission. In this way the gospel of the kingdom has been able to reach its ultimate addressees as foretold in Israel's Scriptures, that is, all human beings.

This leads us to consider the relationship between the people of Israel and Jesus. Jesus appears as an eminent member of that people, which recognized him as such from the beginnings of his public activity; moreover, from the Christian perspective he is a unique member of that people (the Son of God, the Logos incarnate). The New Testament presentation of him, however, shows us how this definitive revelation is produced; his presence does not annul the chosen people but instead, in a way, recapitulates it, so that one could say that Jesus is the definitive Israel. The people acquires its eschatological fullness in the person of Jesus, who thus becomes Israel incarnate.[1]

---

1 Regarding this question, cf. Luis Sánchez-Navarro, *Un cuerpo pleno: Cristo y la personalidad corporativa en la Escritura*, SBMat 4 (Madrid: Universidad San Dámaso, 2021).

C. THE CHURCH AND ISRAEL

How can we understand the existence of the historical Israel in light of our study? We consider this question today after twenty centuries of a long and very often painful history, which we cannot disregard; however, this should not prevent us, out of mutual respect and appreciation, from interpreting New Testament passages.[2] Paul addressed this question in a situation that coincides substantially with our own; at that time the Christian community coexisted with communities of Jews who did not believe in Jesus. The relationship between the Church and the Israel that persists in its own way is not easy, and it generates tension. We can intuit, however, that this is a matter of a fruitful tension. According to the New Testament testimony, the universal openness of the Church—the eschatologically renewed Israel—does not annul the significance of the historical existence of Israel, which constitutes a *mystērion* (Rom 11:25) and as such must be interpreted in light of God's salvific will. Paul gives an audacious response: the Israel that without believing in Jesus remains in the covenant with God is likened to branches that have been cut off of the olive tree, which are not dried up but await—even with life—their final "regrafting" (Rom 11:17–24). John's book of Revelation, in turn, presents the twelve tribes of Israel as the door to the heavenly Jerusalem built on the twelve apostles (Rev 21:12). The response that the New Testament offers us, a true prophecy, therefore involves great hope. This question is also very broad, and it exceeds the limits of our work; nevertheless, the passages that we have examined form an essential reference.

D. A PROPOSAL FOR ALL MANKIND

The universal horizon of Jesus' mission has consequences for our time. The gospel of Jesus Christ is for all nations, for all people, of all times, places,

---

2 See in this respect what Marcheselli affirms in "Il Vangelo di Giovanni nel giudaismo," 329–30, in a section titled, "Fare esegesi in modo responsabile." "In our opinion, however, it is necessary to distinguish between the instance of dialogue with contemporary Judaism and the directly historical and exegetical commitment to the interpretation of the texts; while these two aspects influence each other, we must take care not to lose a sense of their difference" (Marcheselli, 329 n. 89).

and cultures.[3] To question this reality would be to question the gospel itself;
as the Second Vatican Council said in a luminous sentence, "For by His incarnation the Son of God has united Himself in some fashion with every man."[4]
The four Gospels testify to Jesus' will that his preaching reach all human
beings; Paul's letters, along with the other New Testament writings, abound in
this idea, developing it and making it a reality. Thus, from the New Testament
standpoint, there would be no meaning in considering faith in Jesus Christ
on equal footing with the other religions in the world. It would presume a
renunciation of the gospel.

This has a necessary consequence. What Jesus teaches his disciples is not
limited to his contemporary listeners or to the first addressees of the New
Testament writings. The necessary work of interpretation and of adaptation
to diverse epochs should not cloud the original fact: the new life proclaimed
by Jesus is a proposal intended for all people. The gospel of Jesus must not
be devalued by historicist interpretations that empty it of its meaning for
the present, or by mere cultural interpretations that identify it as one more
proposal in a multicultural society. The reason is that the gospel is the way
proposed by Jesus for the free acceptance of each human person, a way that
promises fullness of life. The Church is joyfully responsible for this mission.

E. AN INVITATION TO THE MISSION

The universal call of Jesus' gospel represents, finally, a powerful call to
mission. In Paul's words, "woe to me if I do not preach the gospel!" (1 Cor
9:16). This is a mission that implies, above all, respect for the liberty of those
to whom the preaching of the gospel is addressed; any attempt to impose
the gospel goes against its nature, since the act of faith must be free. Faith, if
it is not free, is not Christian. This mission must be inspired by the conviction that the gospel corresponds to the desire for good and for happiness
that beats in every human heart. Just as in the first century the Church,
the eschatologically renewed Israel, could receive a multitude of gentiles

---

3 Cf. Congregation for the Doctrine of the Faith, *Dominus Iesus: On the Unicity and Salvific
Universality of Jesus Christ and the Church* (Vatican City: LEV, 2000).

4 Vatican Council II, *Gaudium et Spes*, December 7, 1965, no. 22.

coming from paganism and offer them the salvation accomplished by Jesus Christ, so also today many men and women who live "in darkness and in the shadow of death" (cf. Luke 1:79) await this word of salvation. The ancient experience of the Church, which testifies to how people of many different epochs, cultures, and places have received one gospel (according to Matthew, Mark, Luke, and John, and testified by Paul and the rest of the New Testament authors), is a powerful incentive in the work of bringing the gospel to the nations. This work is all the more necessary today, well into the third Christian millennium.

Bibliography

Alonso Schökel, Luis, and Cecilia Carniti. *Salmos: Traducción, introducciones y comentario.* 2 vols. NBE.C. Madrid: Cristiandad, 1991–93.

Alonso Schökel, Luis, and José Luis Sicre Díaz. *Job: Comentario teológico y literario.* 2nd ed. NBE.C. Madrid: Cristiandad, 2002.

Aratus. *Phaenomena.* Edited by Douglas Kidd. CCTC 34. Cambridge: Cambridge University Press, 1997.

Asurmendi Ruiz, Jesús M. "Géneros literarios." Pages 315–22 in *Diccionario del Profetismo bíblico.* Edited by José Luis Barriocanal. Burgos: Monte Carmelo, 2008.

Attridge, Harold W. *Essays on John and Hebrews.* WUNT 264. Tübingen: Mohr Siebeck, 2010.

Ausín Olmos, Santiago. "Pecado." Pages 538–45 in *Diccionario del Profetismo bíblico.* Edited by José Luis Barriocanal. Burgos: Monte Carmelo, 2008.

Backhaus, Knut. *Der sprechende Gott: Gesammelte Studien zum Hebräerbrief.* WUNT 240. Tübingen: Mohr Siebeck, 2009.

Barrett, Charles K. *The Gospel of John and Judaism.* 2nd ed. Philadelphia: Fortress, 1975.

———. *The Gospel According to St. John.* London: SPCK, 1978.

———. *The Acts of the Apostles.* 2 vols. ICC. Edinburgh: T&T Clark, 1994.

Barriocanal, José Luis. *La relectura de la tradición del éxodo en el libro de Amós.* TGST 58. Rome: Editrice Pontificia Università Gregoriana, 2000.

Bauckham, Richard. "The Restoration of Israel in Luke-Acts." Pages 325–70 in *The Jewish World around the New Testament.* Grand Rapids, MI: Baker Academic, 2010.

Beaton, Richard. *Isaiah's Christ in Matthew's Gospel.* SNTSMS 123. Cambridge: Cambridge University Press, 2002.

Beasley-Murray, George R. *Jesus and the Kingdom of God.* Grand Rapids, MI: Eerdmans, 1986.

Beauchamp, Paul, *Ley, Profetas, Sabios: Lectura sincrónica del Antiguo Testamento.* Madrid: Cristiandad, 1977.

———. *Hablar de Escrituras santas: Perfil del lector actual de la Biblia*. Barcelona: Herder, 1989.

———. "Israele e le nazioni fuori e dentro la Chiesa: Lettura di Romani 9–11." Pages 169–207 in *Stili di compimento: Lo Spirito e la lettera nelle Scritture*. Assisi: Citadella, 2007.

Belli, Filippo. "'I Giudei' nel vangelo secondo Giovanni. Come affrontare il problema." *RivB* 50 (2002): 63–75.

———. "'Testimoniada por la ley y los profetas'. Rom 3,21: Pablo y las Escrituras." *RevAg* 43 (2002): 413–26.

———. *Argumentation and Use of Scripture in Romans 9–11*. AnBib 183. Rome: Gregorian & Biblical Press, 2010.

Benedict XVI. "Christ and the Church." General Audience. March 15, 2006.

Beutler, Johannes. *Judaism and the Jews in the Gospel of John*. SubBi 30. Rome: Pontifical Biblical Institute, 2006.

Biguzzi, Giancarlo. *"Io distruggerò questo tempio": Il tempio e il giudaismo nel vangelo di Marco*. 2nd ed. Percorsi culturali. Rome: Urbaniana University Press, 2008.

Bird, Michael F. "Jesus and the Gentiles after Jeremias: Patterns and Prospects." *CurBR* 4 (2005): 83–108.

Blenkinsopp, Joseph. *Isaiah 1–39*. AB 19. New York: Doubleday, 2000.

Bonnard, Pierre. *L'Évangile selon Saint Matthieu*. 2nd ed. CNT 1. Neuchatel: Delachaux & Niestle, 1970.

Bovon, François. *Luke. 3: A Commentary on the Gospel of Luke 19:28–24:53*. Hermeneia. Minneapolis: Fortress, 2012.

Boxall, Ian. "Matthew." Pages 1168–237 in *JBC XXI*.

Brown, Raymond E. *The Gospel According to John (I–XII)*. AB 29. Garden City, NY: Doubleday, 1966.

———. *An Introduction to the New Testament*. ABRL. New York: Doubleday, 1997.

———. *An Introduction to the Gospel of John*. Edited by Francis J. Moloney. ABRL. New York: Doubleday, 2003.

Bruce, Frederick F. *The Acts of the Apostles*. 3rd ed. Grand Rapids, MI: Eerdmans, 1990.

Campbell, William S. "'I Rate All Things as Loss': Paul's Puzzling Accounting System: Judaism as Loss or the Re-evaluation of All Things in Christ?" Pages 39–61 in *Celebrating Paul: Festschrift in Honor of Jerome Murphy-O'Connor, O.P., and Joseph A. Fitzmyer, S.J.* Edited by Peter Spitaler. CBQMS 48. Washington, DC: The Catholic Biblical Association of America, 2011.

Carbajosa, Ignacio. "El Antiguo Testamento, realidad abierta." Pages 21–50 in *Entrar en lo Antiguo: Acerca de la relación entre Antiguo y Nuevo Testamento*. Edited by Ignacio Carbajosa and Luis Sánchez-Navarro. PD 16. Madrid: San Dámaso, 2007.

Castro Sánchez, Secundino. *Evangelio de Juan: Comprensión exegético-existencial*. BTC 2. Madrid: Universidad Pontificia Comillas, 2001.

Charlesworth, James H., ed. *Apocalyptic Literature and Testaments*. Vol. 1 of *The Old Testament Pseudepigrapha*. ABRL. New York: Doubleday 1983.

Childs, Brevard S. *Isaiah*. OTL. Louisville, KY: John Knox, 2001.

Cimosa, Mario. "Pueblo/Pueblos." Pages 1565–80 in *NDTB*.

Collins, Adela Y. "The Book of Revelation." Pages 1855–87 in *JBC XXI*.

Congregation for the Doctrine of the Faith, *Dominus Iesus: On the Unicity and Salvific Universality of Jesus Christ and the Church*. Vatican City: LEV 2000.

Davies, William D., and Dale C. Allison, Jr. *The Gospel According to Saint Matthew*. 3 vols. ICC. Edinburgh: T&T Clark, 1988–97.

DeVries, Simon J. *1 Kings*. WBC 12. Waco, TX: Word Books, 1985.

Dion, Paul-Eugène. *Universalismo religioso en Israel: Desde los orígenes a la crisis macabea*. BNot 3. Estella, Spain: Verbo Divino, 1976.

Downs, David J. *The Offering of the Gentiles: Paul's Collection for Jerusalem in its Chronological, Cultural, and Cultic Contexts*. WUNT Reihe 2/248. Tübingen: Mohr Siebeck, 2008.

Dunn, James D. G. *Jesus Remembered*. Christianity in the Making 1. Grand Rapids, MI: Eerdmans, 2003.

Dupont, Jacques. *Teologia della Chiesa negli Atti degli Apostoli*. CSB 10. Bologna: Dehoniane, 1984.

Estévez López, Elisa. "El endemoniado de Gerasa: estudio histórico-crítico." Pages 57–71 in *Los milagros de Jesús: Perspectivas metodológicas plurales*. Edited by Rafael Aguirre Monasterio. ABE 39. Estella, Spain: Verbo Divino, 2002.

Farmer, William R. *The Last Twelve Verses of Mark*. SNTSMS 25. Cambridge: Cambridge University Press, 1974.

Fitzmyer, Joseph A. *The Gospel According to Luke*. 2 vols. AB 28–28A. New York: Doubleday, 1981–85.

———. *The Acts of the Apostles: A New Translation and Commentary*. AB 31. New Haven: Doubleday, 1998.

Flori, Lorenzo. *Le domande del Vangelo di Giovanni: Analisi narrativa delle questioni presenti in Gv 1–12*. Assisi: Cittadella, 2013.

Fournier, Marianne. *The Episode at Lystra: A Rhetorical and Semiotic Analysis of Acts 14:7–20a*. AmUSt.TR 197. New York: Peter Lang, 1997.

France, Richard T. *The Gospel of Matthew*. NICNT. Grand Rapids, MI: Eerdmans, 2007.

Friedrich, Gerhard. "*Euangelizomai*." Pages 233–6 in *Theological Dictionary of the New Testament*, abridged in one volume by Geoffrey W. Bromiley. Grand Rapids, MI: Eerdmans, 1985.

García Martínez, Florentino. *The Dead Sea Scrolls Translated: The Qumran Texts in English*. 2nd ed. Leiden: Brill, 1994.

García Serrano, Andrés. *The Presentation in the Temple: The Narrative Function of Lk 2:22–39 in Luke-Acts.* AnBib 197. Rome: Gregorian & Biblical Press, 2012.

Gasparro, Lorenzo. *Simbolo e narrazione in Marco: La dimensione simbolica del secondo Vangelo alla luce della pericope del fico di Mc 11,12–25.* AnBib 198. Rome: Gregorian & Biblical Press, 2012.

Gilbert, Maurice. *La Sapienza del cielo. Proverbi, Giobbe, Qohèlet, Siracide, Sapienza.* Cinisello Balsamo: San Paolo, 2005.

———. "Sabiduría." Pages 1711-28 in *NDTB*.

Gillman, John. "The Letter to the Ephesians." Pages 1663–91 in *JBC XXI*.

Gnilka, Joachim. *Das Evangelium nach Markus I–II.* 3rd ed. EKKNT II/1–2. Zurich: Benziger; Neukirchen: Neukirchener, 1989.

———. *Jesus of Nazareth: Message and History.* Peabody, MA: Hendrickson, 1997.

Goldingay, John. *Isaiah.* NIBCOT 13. Peabody, MA: Hendrickson, 2001.

Gomá Civit, Isidro. *El evangelio según San Mateo.* 2 vols. Madrid: Marova, 1966-76.

Granados, Carlos. *El camino del hombre por la mujer: El matrimonio en el Antiguo Testamento.* EstB 49. Estella, Spain: Verbo Divino, 2014.

———. *Deuteronomio.* CP 6. Madrid: BAC, 2017.

Grelot, Pierre. *Les Juifs dans l'Évangile de Jean.* CRB 34. Paris: Gabalda, 1995.

Hill, Andrew E. *Malachi,* AB 25D. New York: Doubleday, 1998.

Infante, Renzo. *Le feste d'Israele nel Vangelo secondo Giovanni.* Cinisello Balsamo: San Paolo, 2010.

Isizoh, Chidi D. *The Resurrected Jesus Preached in Athens: The Areopagus Speech.* Lagos: Ceedee Publications, 1997.

Jeremias, Joachim. *Jesus' Promise to the Nations.* Translated by S. H. Hooke. Naperville, IL: Allenson, 1958.

———. *The Parables of Jesus.* 2nd ed. New York: Scribner's Sons, 1972.

Koet, Bart J. "Isaiah in Luke-Acts." Pages 79–100 in *Isaiah in the New Testament.* Edited by Steve Moyise and Maarten J. J. Menken. NTSI. London: T&T Clark, 2005.

Kraus, Hans-Joachim. *Psalms 60–150.* Minneapolis: Fortress, 1993.

Lee, Hye J. *"Signore, vogliamo vedere Gesù": La conclusione dell'attività pubblica di Gesù secondo Gv 12,20–36.* TGST 124. Rome: Editrice PUG, 2005.

Lichtenberger, Hermann. *Die Apokalypse.* TKNT 23. Stuttgart: Kohlhammer, 2014.

Louw, Johannes P. and Eugene A. Nida. *Greek-English Lexicon of the New Testament,* based on Semantic Domains. Atlanta: Scholars Press, 1988.

Lozano Lozano, Alfonso. *Romanos 5: La vida de los justificados por la fe y su fundamento, la reconciliación por nuestro Señor Jesucristo.* ABE 56. Estella, Spain: Verbo Divino, 2012.

Lukasz, Czeslaw. *Evangelizzazione e conflitto: Indagine sulla coerenza letteraria e tematica della pericope di Cornelio (Atti 10,1–11,18)*. EHS.T 484. Frankfurt am Main: Peter Lang, 1993.

Luz, Ulrich. *Matthew 8–20: A Commentary*. Hermeneia. Minneapolis: Fortress, 2001.

———. *Matthew 21–28: A Commentary*. Hermeneia. Minneapolis: Fortress, 2005.

———. *Matthew 1–7: A Commentary*. Hermeneia. Minneapolis: Fortress, 2007.

Lyonnet, Stanislas. *La historia de la salvación en la carta a los romanos*. Salamanca: Sígueme, 1967.

Mahfouz, Hady. *La fonction littéraire et théologique de Lc 3,1–20 dans Luc-Actes*. USEK.T 11. Kaslik: Université Saint-Esprit, 2003.

Manzi, Franco. *Carta a los Hebreos*. CBJer 6. Bilbao: Desclée de Brouwer, 2005.

Manzo, Juana L. Review of *Una luz para las naciones: La vocación universal del Evangelio*, by Luis Sánchez-Navarro. *CBQ* 80 (2018): 154–55.

Marcheselli, Maurizio. "Il Vangelo di Giovanni nel giudaismo: Un'identità in tensione." *RivB* 61 (2013): 297–330.

Marcus, Joel. *Mark: A New Translation with Introduction and Commentary*. AB 27–27A. New Haven: Yale University Press, 2000–2009.

Markl, Dominik. "Introduction to the Pentateuch." Pages 187–96 in *JBC XXI*.

Matera, Frank J. *New Testament Theology: Exploring Diversity and Unity*. Louisville, KY: John Knox, 2007.

———. *Romans*. Paideia. Grand Rapids, MI: Baker Academic, 2010.

———. *God's Saving Grace: A Pauline Theology*. Grand Rapids, MI: Eerdmans, 2012.

McHugh, John F. *John 1–4*. ICC. London: T&T Clark, 2009.

Meier, John P. *Mentor, Message, and Miracles*. Vol. 2 of *A Marginal Jew: Rethinking the Historical Jesus*. New York: Doubleday, 1994.

Metzger, Bruce M. *A Textual Commentary on the Greek New Testament*. 2nd ed. Stuttgart: Deutsche Bibelgesellschaft, 1994.

Miler, Jean. *Les citations d'accomplissement dans l'Évangile de Matthieu: Quand Dieu se rend présent en toute humanité*. AnBib 140. Rome: Pontificio Istituto Biblico, 1999.

Mitchell, Alan C. "'A Sacrifice of Praise': Does Hebrews Promote Supersessionism?" Pages 251–67 in *Reading the Epistle to the Hebrews: A Resource for Students*. Edited by Eric F. Mason and Kevin B. McCruden. SBLRBS 66. Atlanta: SBL, 2011.

Moloney, Francis J. *The Gospel of John*. SP 4. Collegeville, MN: The Liturgical Press, 1998.

Morla Asensio, Víctor. *Libros sapienciales y otros escritos*. IEB 5. Estella, Spain: Verbo Divino, 1994.

Moyise, Steve. "Is Mark's Opening Quotation the Key to his Use of Scripture?" *IBS* 20 (1998): 146–58.

Muñoz León, Domingo. *Palabra y Gloria: Excursus en la Biblia y en la Literatura Intertestamentaria.* Madrid: CSIC-Instituto "Francisco Suárez," 1983.

———. *Derás: Los caminos y sentidos de la palabra divina en la Escritura. Parte I: Derás targúmico y Derás neotestamentario.* BHB 12. Madrid: CSIC, 1987.

———. "Evangelio según san Juan." Pages 589–682 in *Nuevo Testamento.* Vol. 2 of *Comentario Bíblico Latinoamericano.* Edited by Armando J. Levoratti. Estella, Spain: Verbo Divino, 2003.

Oswalt, John N. *The Book of Isaiah: Chapters 40–66.* NICOT. Grand Rapids, MI: Eerdmans, 1998.

O'Toole, Robert F. *The Unity of Luke's Theology: An Analysis of Luke-Acts.* GNS 9. Wilmington, DE: Glazier, 1984.

Pereira, Francis. *Ephesus: Climax of Universalism in Luke-Acts.* Anand, India: Gujarat Sahitya Prakash, 1983.

Pérez Herrero, Francisco. *Pasión y Pascua de Jesús según san Marcos.* PFTNE.B 67. Burgos: Facultad de Teología del Norte de España, 2001.

Pérez Márquez, Ricardo A. *L'Antico Testamento nell'Apocalisse: Storia della ricerca, bilancio e prospettive.* Assisi: Cittadella, 2010.

Pierron, Joseph and Pierre Grelot. "Nations." Page 380 in *Dictionary of Biblical Theology*, ed. Xavier Léon-Dufour, trans. P. Joseph Cahill S.J., revisions and new articles translated by E. M. Stewart, 2nd ed. (New York: Seabury, 1973).

Pontifical Biblical Commission, *The Jewish People and their Sacred Scriptures in the Christian Bible.* 2001.

Prigent, Pierre. *Commentary on the Apocalypse of St. John.* Tübingen: Mohr Siebeck, 2001.

Rahlfs, Alfred. *Psalmi cum Odis.* 2nd ed. Septuaginta X. Göttingen: Vandenhoeck & Ruprecht, 1967.

Ramis, Francesc. *Isaías.* 2 vols. CBJer 19A–B. Bilbao: Desclée de Brouwer, 2006–8.

———. "El ocaso del mal: Is 19,16–25." Pages 191–215 in *Weodî (immak: Aún me quedas tú: Homenaje a Vicente Collado Bertomeu.* Edited by Juan Miguel Díaz Rodelas, Miguel Pérez Fernández, and Fernando Ramón Casas. Estella, Spain: Verbo Divino, 2009.

Ratzinger, Joseph (Benedict XVI). *Jesus of Nazareth: From the Baptism in the Jordan to the Transfiguration.* Translated by Adrian J. Walker. New York: Doubleday, 2007.

———. *Jesus of Nazareth: Holy Week: From the Entrance into Jerusalem to the Resurrection.* Translated by Philip J. Whitmore. San Francisco: Ignatius Press, 2011.

———. *Jesus of Nazareth: The Infancy Narratives.* Translated by Philip J. Whitmore. New York: Image, 2012.

Ravasi, Gianfranco. *Salmi 51–100.* Vol. 2 of *Il Libro del Salmi: Commento e attualizzazione.* Bologna: Dehoniane, 1985.

Rodríguez Carmona, Antonio. *Evangelio de Mateo.* CBJer 1ª. Bilbao: Desclée de Brouwer, 2006.

Roloff, Jürgen. *Hechos de los Apóstoles*. BBC. Madrid: Cristiandad, 1984.

Romero Sánchez, Luis Manuel. *La eficacia liberadora de la Palabra de Jesús: La intención pragmática de Mc 5,1–20 en su contexto lingüístico y situacional*. ABE 49. Estella, Spain: Verbo Divino, 2009.

Ronning, John. *The Jewish Targums and John's Logos Theology*. Peabody, MA: Hendrickson, 2010.

Sánchez Bosch, Jordi. *Maestro de los pueblos: Una teología de Pablo, el apóstol*. Estella, Spain: Verbo Divino, 2007.

Sánchez-Navarro, Luis. *La Enseñanza de la Montaña: Comentario contextual a Mateo 5–7*. EstB 27. Estella, Spain: Verbo Divino, 2005.

———. "La Escritura para las naciones: Acerca del universalismo en Mateo." *ScrTh* 40 (2008): 525–41.

———. "Cristo y la paraclesis en Pablo." Pages 167–85 in *Pablo y Cristo. La centralidad de Cristo en el pensamiento de san Pablo*. Edited by Luis Sánchez-Navarro. Cmat 5. Madrid: San Dámaso, 2009.

———. *Testimonios del Reino: Evangelios sinópticos y Hechos de los Apóstoles*. Madrid: Palabra, 2010.

———. *Un cuerpo pleno: Cristo y la personalidad corporativa en la Escritura*. SBMat 4. Madrid: Universidad San Dámaso, 2021.

Schlier, Heinrich. *Carta a los Efesios: Comentario*. BEB 71. Salamanca: Sígueme, 1991.

Schlosser, Jacques. *Le groupe des Douze: Les lueurs de l'histoire*. LB 184. Paris: Cerf, 2014.

Schnackenburg, Rudolf. *The Gospel According to St. John*. 3 vols. HTCNT. London: Burns & Oates, 1968–82.

Simoens, Yves. *Apocalisse di Giovanni, Apocalisse di Gesù Cristo: Una traduzione e un'interpretazione*. Bologna: Dehoniane, 2010.

Soards, Marion L. *The Speeches in Acts: Their Content, Context, and Concerns*. Louisville, KY: John Knox, 1994.

Stock, Klemens. *Boten aus dem Mit-Ihm-Sein: Das Verhältnis zwischen Jesus und den Zwölf nach Markus*. AnBib 70. Rome: Biblical Institute Press, 1975.

———. *Gesù il Figlio di Dio: Il messaggio di Giovanni*. BibPr 16. Rome: Edizioni ADP, 1993.

———. *Marco: Commento contestuale al secondo Vangelo*. BibPr 47. Rome: ADP, 2003.

———. *La última palabra es de Dios: El Apocalipsis como Buena Noticia*. Madrid: San Pablo, 2005.

Svartvik, Jesper. "Leggere la Lettera agli Ebrei senza presupporre la teologia della sostituzione." Pages 129–47 in *Gesù Cristo e il popolo ebraico: Interrogativi per la teologia di oggi*. Edited by Philip A. Cunningham. BibDial 5. Rome: Gregorian & Biblical Press, 2012.

Tatum, G., "'To the Jew First' (Romans 1:16): Paul's Defense of Jewish Privilege in Romans." Pages 275–86 in *Celebrating Paul: Festschrift in Honor of Jerome Murphy-O'Connor,*

O.P., and Joseph A. Fitzmyer, S.J. Edited by Peter Spitaler. CBQMS 48. Washington, DC: The Catholic Biblical Association of America, 2011.

Taylor, Vincent. *The Gospel According to St. Mark.* 2nd ed. London: McMillan, 1966.

Thielman, Frank. *Ephesians.* BECNT. Grand Rapids, MI: Baker Academic, 2010.

Thiessen, Jacob. *Gott hat Israel nicht verstoßen: Biblisch-exegetische Perspektiven in der Verhältnisbestimmung von Israel, Judentum und Gemeinde Jesu.* EDIS 3. Frankfurt am Main: Peter Lang, 2010.

Thyen, Hartwig. "Johannesevangelium." *TRE* 17 (1988): 200–225.

Tisera, Guido. *Universalism According to the Gospel of Matthew.* EHS.T 482. Frankfurt am Main: Peter Lang, 1993.

Trilling, Wolfgang. *Das Wahre Israel: Studien zur Theologie des Matthäus-Evangeliums.* 3rd ed. SANT 10. München: Kösel-Verlag, 1964.

Vanhoye, Albert. "Salut universel par le Christ et validité de l'Ancienne Alliance." *NRTh* 116 (1994): 815–35.

———. *The Letter to the Hebrews: A New Commentary.* Translated by Leo Arnold. New York: Paulist, 2015.

Vanni, Ugo. *Apocalisse e Antico Testamento: Una sinossi.* 2nd ed. Rome: Pontificio Istituto Biblico, 1987.

———. *Lectura del Apocalipsis: Hermenéutica, exégesis, teología.* Estella, Spain: Verbo Divino, 2005.

Vatican Council II. *Dei Verbum.* November 18, 1965.

———. *Gaudium et Spes.* December 7, 1965.

von Rad, Gerhard. *Wisdom in Israel.* Translated by James D. Martin. London: SCM Press, 1972.

Wagner, J. Ross. "Isaiah in Romans and Galatians." Pages 117–32 in *Isaiah in the New Testament.* Edited by Steve Moyise and Maarten J. J. Menken. NTSI. London: T&T Clark, 2005.

Walter, Nikolaus. "ἔθνος." *EDNT* 1:381–83.

Wengst, Klaus. *Das Johannesevangelium. 1. Teilband: Kapitel 1–10.* TKNT 4/1. Stuttgart: Kohlhammer, 2000.

Wilson, Stephen G. *The Gentiles and the Gentile Mission in Luke-Acts.* SNTSMS 23. Cambridge: Cambridge University Press, 1973.

Zerwick, Max. *The Epistle to the Ephesians.* Translated by Kevin Smyth. New York: Herder and Herder, 1969.

Scriptural Index

General Index